D0819971

a canon of vegetables

Also by Raymond Sokolov

a canon of
vegetables

101 classic recipes

raymond sokolov

WILLIAM MORROW
An Imprint of HarperCollinsPublishers

HarperCollins books may be purchased for educational, business, or sales promotional use. For information please write: Special Markets Department, HarperCollins Publishers, 10 East 53rd Street, New York, NY 10022.

FIRST EDITION

Designed by rlf design

Library of Congress Cataloging-in-Publication Data

Sokolov, Raymond A.
    A canon of vegetables: 101 classic recipes / Raymond Sokolov.
      p.   cm.
    Includes bibliographical references and index.
    ISBN: 978-0-06-072582-2
    ISBN-10: 0-06-072582-6
    1. Cookery (Vegetables).   2. Cookery, International.   I. Title.   II. Title: A canon of vegetables.

TX801.S6145   2007
641.6'5—dc22

                                              2006046865

07 08 09 10 11 WBC/RRD 10 9 8 7 6 5 4 3 2 1

To Susan Friedland

contents

acknowledgments

Susan Friedland commissioned this book as a sequel to *The Cook's Canon,* which she also published. While it would be churlish to begrudge her the pleasures of leisure, I can say that I am one of many authors who miss her guidance. On the other hand, if she had not decided to cultivate her penthouse garden in Greenwich Village, I would not have come under the tutelage of Hugh Van Dusen, a true Harper perennial and a gent with deep roots in the world of books. Once again I have to thank Kathy Robbins for negotiating a steady course between the demands of life and work.

introduction

This is not a vegetarian cookbook. It is a compendium of great recipes in which vegetables from all over the world play a leading role. Like its predecessor, *The Cook's Canon,* it contains 101 classic recipes every informed cook should know about. My ruling principle in making this personal—but I hope not capricious—selection was the same as for the earlier collection: to winnow 101 recipes into a plausible pantheon of the most brilliant, influential, delicious, and enduring vegetable dishes human beings had created since they learned to cook.

This is also not a primer of basic techniques for cooking vegetables. Some of the recipes are very basic indeed, but they are here because they are remarkable conceptions, remarkable to prepare and remarkable to eat.

My professional interest in vegetables, as a gastronomic writer and historian, began thirty years ago, when I annoyed the editor of *Natural History* magazine, Alan Ternes, with a column on cannibalism from the consumer's point of view. It was based on ethnographic reports and ended with a recipe for *pain de cervelles,* an haute cuisine "brain loaf" whose main ingredient was specified as coming from any higher mammal. Alan saw this sort of anthropological jape as a dead end. "Anthropology isn't a real science anyway," he said over lunch at a dismal Upper West Side Manhattan restaurant near the American Museum of Natural History, which then published *Natural History.* "Why don't you switch your focus to botany?"

"I don't know anything about botany," I said.

"You will," he said, grinning. "Soon. Your next deadline is only two weeks off."

For the next eighteen years, I followed his advice and mostly avoided the relatively limited menagerie of edible fauna for the infinitely ramified and fascinating domain of plants. At a certain point, I realized that I was a journalist within a scientific field—economic botany—plants in human affairs. There is no broader or more important subject.

My past as a science writer and as a classicist has shaped this book. The history of cultivated plants and their names is everywhere in these pages. But my goal is not so much to teach as to delight, to give vegetables their historic, social, and scientific due, to ennoble them while also celebrating the sensual qualities that have brought them to the table over millennia.

For botanists, "vegetable" is a clearly defined technical term, quite separate from "fruit." For cooks and eaters, the distinction is less precise but easy to understand in practice. Botanically, a fruit is a plant's sexual part, the organ with the seeds. The rest of the plant is vegetable—roots, stems, leaves, and so forth. This does not mean that plants always reproduce sexually. But when they spread through root systems or grafts, or when gardeners put cuttings in soil, this is called vegetative reproduction. It is often the best way to "reproduce" a plant exactly, since it does not mix the genome of two parents—the essence of sexual reproduction—but preserves the genetic makeup of a single plant whose qualities have recommended it to a human grower. Without vegetative reproduction, agriculture would be unpredictable, in fact nearly impossible, since you could never know what crop you would be getting. Farming would be a crapshoot instead of a scientific improvement on nomadic hunting and gathering.

As you see, I still haven't lost my penchant for anthropology. Or, as I would prefer to call it, my reflex to stress the human side of economic botany. And it is precisely the human element—common sense—that trumps the neat botanical categories of vegetable and fruit. Botanists themselves, in my experience, are quite ready to follow ordinary usage where a strict adherence to professional terminology would only spread confusion and consternation. Even at a lunch exclusively attended by botanists, you would not be likely to hear anyone call a tomato a fruit. Although it is a fruit in the parlance of botany. Only lay pedants insist on pointing out that tomatoes have seeds, as do peppers, beans, okra, squash, and cucumber.

The banana is a textbook example of all these tangled considerations. The "banana" we buy in groceries, with its yellow peel and soft fleshy pulp, is a fruit from any perspective. Botanists go a step further and call it a berry because it has a skin and a soft, seed-bearing interior. Except that cultivated bananas don't have seeds, just their remnants, tiny black spots visible when the fruit is sliced. Cultivated banana plants reproduce vegetatively, from fleshy underground "corms" (fleshy stems easy to mix up with bulbs, which are buds). Furthermore, an economically important variety of banana, the plantain or cooking banana, is almost always considered a vegetable by those who consume it.

In the end, eaters decide what is a vegetable and what is not. Speaking broadly, fruits are sweet and soft and mostly can be eaten out of hand, or in desserts and specific fruit dishes. Vegetables, even the ones that are technically fruits, are most often eaten either raw in salads or cooked as part of the main meal. Anyone can think of exceptions. There is always tomato ice cream to upset the applecart of sensible discussion.

I have never met anyone who did not intuitively understand all of this. So on with the show. Enjoy it. Disagree with the choices of recipes. But cook them before you throw this book in the compost heap.

artichokes

Eating an artichoke *(Cynara scolymus)* is a war of attrition against a thistle, actually a cultivated, immature thistle flower, but a thistle nonetheless. There are artichokes, especially tiny ones, called *carciofini* in Italy, that can be eaten in their entirety, leaves and all. The famous flattened and deep-fried *carciofini alla Giudea* of the Roman ghetto are the leading example of this, and would be included here except that the requisite artichokes are almost never available away from the Mediterranean birthplace of the plant.

The globe (as opposed to the completely unrelated Jerusalem and Chinese artichokes*) artichokes most commonly served everywhere are fist-sized or larger and must be tackled leaf by leaf.[†] At the base of each leaf is a soft half-moon of

5

edible flesh torn from the fleshy base, or *fond*. Once you have worked your way through this palisade of bracts,[‡] you come to the hairy and inedible choke, which must be scraped away before the deliciously earthy and dense discoid bottom can be cut up, dipped in melted butter (if hot) or vinaigrette (if cold), and eaten with the pleasure that comes from enjoying a hard-won and thoroughly desirable prize.

*The Jerusalem artichoke (*Helianthus tuberosus*) is botanically a sunflower native to North America. Invasive with a capital I, it will choke other plants out of gardens. The edible part, a knobby tuber, has an appealing nutty flavor but did not inspire any great recipes until Michel Troisgros and Daniel Boulud created soups from it. The name is most plausibly a distortion of the Italian word for sunflower, *girasole*. The French name, *topinambour*, derives from the Amazonian people known as Tupinamba. This is a puzzle worth exploring, since the plant was introduced into France from Canada by Samuel Champlain (1567–1635), he of the great lake that divides New York from Vermont. The Chinese, or sometimes the Japanese, artichoke is also a tuber. Escoffier, who called it *crosne du Japon*,[§] advised treating it like a regular artichoke. I have never seen one.

[†]A process that inspired the Italian expression *la politica del carciofo*, a tactic of picking off your opponents one at a time.

[‡]Bracts are modified leaves associated with flowers, as for example the red, pink, or white "petals" of the poinsettia.

[§]After the French village near Corbeil, itself a center of flour milling and birthplace of the Homer scholar Jean-Baptiste d'Ansse de Villoison (1753–1805), whose last name means Gosling Town. Since his birthplace means basket, it is curiously fitting that his middle name means basket handle.

artichoke soup

If you want to venture beyond this basic *politica del carciofo*, and avoid fooling with the choke at the table, here is a laborious but brilliant way to go. The soup is powerfully intense in taste. It will also be fiberless and silken if you take the trouble to push it through a very fine sieve.

4 medium artichokes
1 lemon, cut into quarters
6 tablespoons butter
2 medium potatoes, peeled and thickly sliced
Salt and pepper
6½ to 7 cups chicken stock

1. Cut off the stem end of each artichoke. Then cut them in half from top to bottom. Rub the cut surfaces with the lemon to inhibit discoloration from contact with the air. Cut out the hairy choke and discard. Brush any new cuts with lemon.

2. In a small saucepan, bring 3 cups of water to a boil.

3. While this is happening, melt the butter in a Dutch oven. When the foam subsides, add the artichokes and toss them in the butter so that all exposed surfaces are coated. Pour the boiling water over them. When the water returns to the boil, lower the heat, cover, and simmer for a half hour, or until the artichoke bottoms are barely tender.

4. Add the potato slices, season to taste with the salt and pepper, and continue to simmer, covered, until the potatoes are soft. Remove the artichoke pieces to one bowl with a slotted spoon and the potato slices to another.

5. Scrape all the edible flesh from the bottom ends of all the artichoke leaves. Add the scrapings to the potato slices. Trim the artichoke bottoms and cut them in quarters.

6. Process the artichoke scrapings and the potatoes, adding as much cooking liquid to the processor jar as is necessary to speed the conversion of the artichoke and potato mixture into a smooth puree.

7. Scrape the puree into a mixing bowl. Whisk in the remaining cooking liquid. Then force the mixture through a chinois or other fine strainer into a clean bowl. Whisk in as much chicken stock as you need to get the consistency you want. At this point you can refrigerate the soup. It can be served chilled, at room temperature, or reheated.

Serves 4

artichokes à la barigoule
stuffed artichokes

Artichauts à la barigoule are stuffed with the condensed mushroom paste called Duxelles (page 155) and sauced with a reduction of their cooking liquid. Barigoule is the vernacular name of a kind of mushroom gathered in southeast France.

6 medium artichokes

1 lemon, quartered

½ pound mushrooms, trimmed and finely chopped

3 tablespoons butter

2 tablespoons oil

1 medium onion, peeled and finely chopped, for the duxelles

1 garlic clove, peeled and finely chopped

4 ounces salt pork, grated or chopped

Salt and pepper

1 large carrot, scraped and sliced in ¼-inch rounds

2 small onions, peeled and thinly sliced

¼ pound fresh pork rind

1 bay leaf

2 thyme sprigs

2 parsley sprigs

12 very thin strips of salt pork, 5 by 2½ inches

1 cup dry white wine

3 cups veal stock or beef bouillon

1. Trim the artichokes. Rub all cut surfaces with the lemon quarters. First, snap off the stem and then slice the bottom to level it. Twist off the small leaves at the bottom and discard. Lay the artichokes on their sides and slice off the top two inches of the leaves, leaving a flat level surface. Cut away the tips of the lower leaves. Reach into the interior of the artichokes and pull out the papery, violet leaves at the center to expose the furry choke. With a grapefruit spoon, scoop and scrape out the choke completely. Don't forget to rub the exposed top of the artichoke bottom with a piece of lemon. Set the trimmed artichokes aside.

2. Prepare a duxelles stuffing, following the directions on page 155 for squeezing liquid out of the mushrooms. Heat 1 tablespoon of the butter with the oil and sauté the onion and garlic in it until the onion is translucent. Beat in the chopped mush-

rooms and stir them together with the onion and garlic. Keep stirring over medium heat to cook the mushrooms and let their remaining liquid steam away. Remove from the heat and let the duxelles cool until still hot but comfortable to the touch. Beat in the grated or chopped salt pork. Season to taste with salt and pepper.

3. There should be about 1½ tablespoons of duxelles stuffing per artichoke. Place one-eighth of the total inside each artichoke on top of the bottom. Smear the insides of the leaves with one-sixth of the remaining duxelles.

4. Melt the remaining butter in a small skillet and sauté the carrot rounds and onion slices until they are lightly browned.

Take a saucepan large enough to hold the artichokes comfortably in a single layer standing up. Spread the pork rind (fat side down) on the bottom of the saucepan. Spread the rind with the carrot rounds and onion slices, the bay leaf, the thyme, and the parsley. Pull up the ends of the salt pork strips and tie around the artichokes with a string, so as to make the 8 artichokes into a single package.

5. Then put in the artichokes. Pour in the white wine and bring to a boil. Continue boiling, uncovered, until the wine has reduced to about 3 tablespoons. Then pour in the stock or bouillon. It should come up about halfway on the artichokes. Add water if the quantity of the stock is insufficient to reach this height.

6. Bring the liquid to a boil, cover, and set over low-medium heat so that it bubbles away slowly and without interruption for 45 minutes. After 30 minutes, uncover so that the lower part of the salt pork wrapping will brown.

7. Set the artichokes on a serving platter. Cut the strings and discard. Remove the salt pork, trim away the unbrowned portion, and discard. Trim the reserved salt pork pieces into squares and put them on a plate in a low oven to keep them warm. Put the serving platter with the artichokes in there, too.

8. Strain the cooking liquid through a chinois into a saucepan. Let it stand for a few minutes so that the fat rises and can be sponged away with paper toweling. Measure the liquid. If there is more than 2½ cups, bring to a boil and reduce to that amount.

9. Strain the liquid through the chinois a second time into a clean bowl and pour over the artichokes. Then set a browned square of salt pork on top of each artichoke and serve.

Serves 6

escabeche of vegetables
cold braised vegetables in vinegar sauce

All around the Mediterranean, escabeche is a prized method of preserving food, mainly fish, in a two-part process that goes back at least to the medieval Arabs, who brought it to Europe from wherever they found it. Step one is frying the food in olive oil. Step two is immersing it in a vinegar sauce.

The word "escabeche" may be a linguistic ancestor to ceviche, that New World preparation of raw fish "cooked" heatlessly in acid citrus juice. We know that "escabeche" itself goes back to an Arabic original, hispanicized—or catalanized—and written down in Spain in the fourteenth century. In her article on the subject in *Petits Propos Culinaires* (No. 20, 1985), Barbara Santich refers to a total of four medieval recipes from the Mediterranean region, all with typically medieval sweet-and-sour flavorings, such as almonds, currants, and dates, to balance the vinegar. But escabeche is no antique relic. Venerable, yes, yet still a staple from Barcelona to Istanbul. Put a grave accent on the second *e* and the same dish is French. In our day, the dish has evolved away from its origins, losing the sweetness but keeping the vinegar.

Actually, escabeche is less an individual dish than a method, a method that can be applied to a whole range of foods other than fish. Here I offer a sumptuous vegetable escabeche. In our day, the dish has evolved away from its origins, with a bit of nutmeg for a hint of its original medieval spicing. The next day—escabeches are meant to be eaten the next day or later on, and they will taste better for the wait—serve it cold, as a first course. Escabeches are ideal for warm weather, the climate they were invented for long ago, when the role of vinegar was much larger than it is now.

1 lemon, cut in half

8 small artichokes

3 tablespoons kosher salt

1 head broccoli, blanched

1 cauliflower, blanched

2 cups olive oil

8 garlic cloves, peeled

2 medium onions, peeled and sliced into ¼-inch rings

3 large carrots, scraped and cut into rounds

2 pickled (canned or bottled) jalapeño peppers, seeded and cut into matchstick strips

1 bay leaf

12 black peppercorns

12 oregano sprigs or 1 teaspoon dried oregano

½ teaspoon ground or (preferably) grated whole nutmeg

1 cup red wine vinegar

1 bottle white wine

1. Fill a bowl with 2 quarts of cold water. Squeeze half the lemon into it.

2. Trim the artichokes: Snap off the stems. Cut away the outer skin of the stems and drop in the water. With a knife, level the bottoms of the artichokes. Rub the bottoms with the squeezed lemon half. Cut off the first inch of the tops of the leaves. Pull off the small leaves at the bottom. With a scissors, cut off the points on the remaining whole leaves. As you make these cuts, rub with the lemon.

3. Slice the artichokes in half lengthwise. Remove the fuzzy chokes and put the cleaned halves into the salted water with the stems.

4. Bring 4 quarts of water to a boil. Add 1 tablespoon of the salt and the juice of the remaining half-lemon. Add the squeezed lemon halves and the artichoke halves, and cook for 30 minutes, or until they are just tender. Remove from the water with a slotted spoon and let drain, cut sides down, on a rack.

5. Cut the broccoli and cauliflower into flowerets.

6. In a large flameproof earthenware casserole or other heavy large pot, heat the olive oil. Add the garlic and sauté over medium heat for a second or two. Then add the onions, carrots, jalapeño pepper strips, bay leaf, peppercorns, chopped (or dried), oregano, nutmeg, and the remaining 2 tablespoons salt. Stir-fry for 2 minutes.

7. Add the artichokes, broccoli, and cauliflower. Stir-fry for 1 minute. Then pour in the vinegar and white wine. Mix well, bring to a boil, reduce the heat, and simmer for 5 minutes. Remove from the heat and let cool to room temperature. Remove the bay leaf before serving. Serve. Or refrigerate in a tightly covered vessel for as long as a week, before serving at room temperature.

Serves 12

asparagus

My happiest asparagus moment came at lunch with Gael Greene, a fellow Detroiter who was looking me over and trying to come to terms with my arrival on her turf at *New York* magazine. We already knew each other, and we seemed to be getting on perfectly well, on a sunny day in 1980. Gael had ordered asparagus and passed her plate across to me so that I could have a taste. While I cut into the bright green spears, we went on talking. We continued to discuss my brilliant future at *New York* (which actually lasted only a few months before I took an offer to edit *Book Digest* for Dow Jones) and I began to eat asparagus. After a certain point, Gael looked down and moaned: "You've eaten all the tips."

It was true. I had absentmindedly consumed all the tender tips and left behind the woody stalks. To Gael's credit, she recovered her good nature. When her current boyfriend, a well-known porn actor, just happened to walk up to our table, she introduced me as "my brilliant new colleague and a great asparagus lover."*

That I am. Wild asparagus, white asparagus, thin asparagus, fat asparagus—I am passionate about all varieties of *Asparagus officinalis*, a member of the lily family known in Europe since ancient times. The season used to be be limited to April and May in Europe and the U.S. Northeast, but California extended that by several months. And now Peru fills in the gaps with excellent asparagus all winter (ours, not theirs). Critics of globalism can caterwaul as much as they like, but a system that makes high-quality asparagus available year-round sustains my enthusiasm.

My friend George Lang is probably the world's greatest asparagophile. He collects asparagus plates and china, creates asparagus graphics, and has been known to serve an all-asparagus menu at his restaurant near Lincoln Center in Manhattan, the Cafe des Artistes. But even he would agree that the ideal asparagus dish is not a soup or a soufflé or even asparagus with prosciutto. It is plain asparagus, artfully trimmed and lightly steamed, then filmed with butter.

Madame Saint-Ange, the author of the best French cookbook ever written (with typical self-confidence, she called it *La Cuisine de Madame Saint-Ange*), devotes two densely packed pages to this "simple" procedure.

The trimming alone occupies her for a few hundred words. *Bref*, cut away any isolated leaves along the stems and then peel them, immersing them in cold water as you go. Drain and then sort by thickness into bundles of six, eight, or ten, according to their size. Tie each bundle with two pieces of string, one 2 inches below the tips, the second 3 inches farther down the stems. Then arrange the bundles side by side so that the points are all on an even line. Finally, with one stroke of a large knife, slice away the bottoms of the stems, leaving all the bundles the same length, around 7 inches.

*Gael herself entered the "adult" industry as a novelist in 1976, with the brilliantly titled *Blue Skies, No Candy*.

There is a point to all of this fuss. The sorting makes it easy to cook all the asparagus evenly. The peeling and cutting eliminate inedible fibrous areas. And the tying helps prevent damage to the tips when you move the cooked asparagus out of the pot and onto the serving dish.

And what about the pot? Even well-ordered homes do not often have a purpose-built *boîte à asperges*, a 10-inch-tall cylindrical pot with a basket that fits inside and will extract cooked asparagus as gently as the perforated rack in a fish poacher removes a whole bass without harming it. What matters is that the asparagus be completely submerged in lots of water—7 cups per pound, lightly salted.

Bring this water to a full rolling boil and plunge in the asparagus. Do not cover. When boiling resumes, reduce the heat to produce a moderate, regular bubbling. Cook medium asparagus for 12 minutes after boiling resumes. Thin asparagus take less time, thick ones more. Test with a knife point. Overcooking is a sin. Better to have just a bit of snap left than to let them slide into insipid flaccidity.

Drain off the asparagus cooking liquid. Place the bundles on a dry clean dishcloth while they drip-dry. Transfer to a long serving dish lined with a white cloth. Carefully cut and remove the strings. Serve with melted butter or, for a grander effect, hollandaise. For cold asparagus, use a vinaigrette or mayonnaise.

For most of us, most of the time, that is all we need to know about asparagus cookery. Madame Saint-Ange does not include any other asparagus recipes, except for a similarly plain treatment of delicate green asparagus. In the absence of a truly paramount classic asparagus dish (as opposed to the very classic preparation outlined above), I offer my version of a Georgian asparagus soup and a recipe for asparagus risotto, notable because it substitutes asparagus cooking liquid for the usual light meat broth, exploiting the flavor of the asparagus with exemplary frugality, not to mention the added convenience.

asparagus soup

This is an adaptation of the traditional Georgian spring soup *satatsuri* (as recorded by Darra Goldstein in her authoritative *Georgian Feast*). My version purees the asparagus, uses chicken stock instead of water, and offers a choice of cilantro or parsley, instead of a mixture of the two combined with dill. Since cilantro is a Georgian favorite, it gives the soup a pure regional taste, and also serves as an excellent complement to the asparagus. Add the cilantro at the last minute or the flavor will swoon away in the twinkling of a simmer.

2 pounds asparagus
4 tablespoons butter
2 medium onions, peeled and finely chopped
8 to 10 cups chicken stock
1 tablespoon salt
Pepper
4 eggs
½ cup chopped cilantro or parsley

1. Cut away the woody ends of the asparagus. Cut into inch-long pieces. Reserve the tips.

2. Melt 2 tablespoons of the butter in a 2-quart saucepan. When the foaming subsides, add the inch-long asparagus pieces and the onions. Sauté for 3 minutes, stirring occasionally. Add the stock to cover, bring to a boil, reduce the heat, and simmer until the asparagus are completely soft, about 5 minutes.

3. Process until smooth. Return to the (cleaned) saucepan. Add the remaining butter, all the remaining stock except for 2 cups, and salt and pepper to taste.

4. When ready to serve, bring to a boil and reduce the heat so that the soup barely bubbles. If you want a thinner soup, add the remaining stock and return to the simmer. Add the asparagus tips.

5. Without hesitation (the asparagus tips should cook only a minute or two), put the eggs in a bowl. Whisk until smooth. Then whisk in 2 tablespoons of soup. And, finally, whisk the egg mixture into the soup. The egg is supposed to coagulate, as in a Chinese egg drop soup or the Roman standby stracciatella.

6. Remove from the heat, stir in the chopped cilantro or parsley, and serve immediately.

Serves 6 to 8

asparagus risotto

1 pound asparagus, prepared in the manner of Madame Saint-Ange (see page 13)

8 tablespoons (1 stick) butter

2 cups Arborio or other medium-grain rice

¼ cup freshly grated Parmesan cheese

Salt and pepper

1. Remove the asparagus from the cooking water (but RESERVE the water) and cut into inch-long pieces. Discard the woody ends, but peel any sections whose interior flesh is edible. Reserve the spears.

2. Measure the cooking water. Top up to 5 cups with additional water if necessary and return to the boil. Reduce the heat and simmer slowly.

3. In a heavy 10-cup pot, melt 6 tablespoons of the butter over medium-high heat. When the foaming subsides, add the asparagus pieces and any pith you have salvaged (but not the spears). Stir-fry for 2 minutes. Then pour in all the rice and stir vigorously to coat each grain. Continue stirring briefly. The grains will turn opaque. Then pour in a cup of the asparagus cooking water. Stir until the liquid almost disappears. Then add another cup of water. Continue in this manner until the rice softens to the al dente point. If you run out of water, bring another cup or two to the boil.

4. As the water-absorption process comes to a close, melt the remaining 2 tablespoons butter in a small skillet. Toss the asparagus spears in the butter to warm them up. Set them aside on a warm plate. Pour the butter into the rice. Add the cheese and salt and pepper to taste and stir vigorously while the cheese melts. Transfer to a serving bowl. Arrange the asparagus spears over the rice and serve immediately.

Serves 6

beans

Pythagoras, apostle of the hypotenuse, forbade his followers to eat beans. Why? Because they reminded him of testicles and because they produce flatulence. Eating symbolic testicles was metaphorical cannibalism of a particularly noxious sort: patiophagy, fatherfeeding. Farting was an even more obvious transgression. We moderns don't like it any more than Pythagoras. Consider the ironic childhood jingle:

> *Beans, beans, the musical fruit,*
> *The more you eat, the more you toot.*
> *The more you toot, the better you feel,*
> *So let's have beans at every meal.*

There is much scientific truth in this jaunty quatrain. Beans and other "windy" foods are rich in oligosaccharides, large-moleculed sugars that pass through the stomach undigested into the large intestine, where bottom-feeding bacteria break them down and release gases as a by-product. The gases create bloating, whose release makes you feel better.

It is also the case, as the poem declares, that beans are fruits. Their pods contain seeds. Indeed, beans are all fruits of the pea family, Leguminosae. So far, so simple. As usual, human contact brings complexity to the plant world. We call them vegetables and we consider them beans whether we are eating their immature pods (green beans, snap beans, bean pods), their seeds, both fresh (limas, favas) and dried (kidney beans, navy beans) or their sprouts.

Most edible beans are members of the New World genus *Phasellus*. Favas, or broad beans, are an Old World species, *Vicia faba*, not closely related except visually to lima beans (*P. lunatus*), which really did originate in Peru (or at least were first seen there by Europeans). Soybeans (*Glycine max*) are, unsurprisingly, of Asian origin.

Excellent fresh green beans are now a year-round staple. The Korean grocer at my corner tops and tails them daily; so I have no excuse not to have them fresh often. Under such circumstances, why would anyone buy canned or frozen beans? But people do, even when fresh beans are at their cheapest in the summer. I know this because I once lurked in the canned vegetable aisle of a Manhattan supermarket all morning interviewing customers who selected canned green beans. They just liked them that way.

This taught me two things. If you accustom someone to an objectively awful food early in life, she will think of it as the natural form, while scorning the fresh version as weird and undesirable. Second, a dubious-looking fellow like me can hang out for hours in a supermarket aisle without arousing suspicion. Moreover, young women do not recoil when he asks them about their food preferences.

In the classic method of cooking green beans (*haricots verts*) taught at the Cordon Bleu in Paris and by its most successful graduate, Julia Child, you bring a large quantity of lightly salted water to the boil and then plunge in the beans. Because there is so much water, it resumes boiling quickly, without stultifying the beans, and as soon as they turn a bright green, they are ready to "refresh" under cold water to stop the cooking and await quick reheating in butter. All this takes place, like nude sunbathing, uncovered. Why? For the same basic reason that you plunge green beans (and other green vegetables) into large quantities of boiling water. To keep them green. For as Harold McGee points out in his magisterial *On Food and Cooking, The Science and Lore of the Kitchen*, heat breaches plant cell walls, releases naturally occurring plant acids, and allows them to break down chlorophyll in a process that alters its color in the dull yellow-green direction. Lots of water has the effect of diluting those acids. High heat, another result of abundant water, kills the enzyme chlorophyllase, which acts on chlorophyll biochemically and increases its vulnerability to attack, thrives in medium-hot water but "dies" in boiling water. In the first few minutes of boiling, some plant acids escape into the air. If there is a cover on the pot, they condense on it and fall back into the pot.

All of this applies equally well to fava beans, but they add an additional complexity to the cooking process. Favas, which are very seasonal in the U.S., come in large, velvety pods (which are the cause of much phallic joking in Italy). Unless the favas are very young, it is not enough to remove the pods. You have to take the skins off the beans, too. The most efficient method is to plunge shelled favas into boiling water, count to 25½, and remove them to refreshing cold water. This loosens the skins. When you pull them off, brilliantly green and tender beans are left, ready for the briefest second boil.

caldo gallego
galician white bean soup with greens

In northwest Spain, in the province of Galicia, where Christian pilgrims trek to the shrine of Saint James of Compostela, the signs are written not in Spanish (always referred to here as castellano, or Castilian) but in *galego*, the Galician version of Portuguese. Political autonomy from Madrid and television that speaks *galego* increase the sense of separation from Spain. This heartiest of hearty soups is the Galician poster dish. It is similar to the Tuscan *Ribollita* (page 131), but you don't want to press that point in Lugo or La Coruña. And, besides, the various meats in this soup make a decisive difference.

Is this Galicia somehow connected to the former province of Austria-Hungary of the same name? Some experts propose that they are both (along with other similarly named places across Europe) echoes of Celtic (Gallic) settlement. To add spice to the pot of this discussion, one ought to mention the principal lingering active relic of Austro-Hungarian Galicia, which stretched across a large swath of eastern Europe, from southern Poland south through the Ukraine. That relic would be one of the two main branches of Yiddish, Galitzianer. The other is Litvak, or Lithuanian Yiddish. Neither of these two Jewish cultural factions was entirely comfortable with the other, linguistically or otherwise, but both Litvaks and Galitzianers in their highly self-aware pre-Hitlerian heydays would have rejected any kinship with the Galicians of Spain—if they had known about them.

¾ pound dried white beans, soaked overnight

¼ pound salt pork or pancetta, diced

½ pound deboned veal breast, sliced across the grain in 1-inch strips

1 medium chorizo (about the size of an Italian sausage), cut into 1-inch rounds

1 pound spareribs, sliced into ribs

¼ cup lard

2 cups greens (turnip, mustard, collard, or kale), shredded

1½ pounds potatoes, peeled and thickly sliced

Salt

1. Bring 2½ quarts (10 cups) of water to a boil in a Dutch oven. Add the beans, the salt pork, the veal breast, the chorizo, and the spareribs. When the liquid resumes boiling, add the lard, lower the heat, and simmer, uncovered, for an hour.

2. Add the greens and the potatoes. Salt to taste and continue simmering until the potatoes are soft, about 15 minutes.

3. Remove 1 cup of potatoes and 1 cup of beans. Mash them together and stir back into the soup to thicken it.

Serves 6

fave al guanciale
fava beans with hog jowl

This is Italy's answer to Hoppin' John (page 40), that mixture of black-eyed peas and pork brought to Charleston, S.C., by slaves from Africa.

Some years ago, I was about to leave New York for a brief expedition into the interior of French Guiana. The trip eventually yielded many gastronomic adventures—peccary barbecues by the wild Maroni River, stewed armadillo at a restaurant in Cayenne, and a curiously tasteless mangosteen stolen from a botanical garden in upland Jamaica. In a sense, however, the most riveting incident associated with this sojourn in the tropics occurred shortly before I left New York. It had to do with beans of the most traditional Northern Hemisphere sort, the species known to science as *Vicia faba*, England's broad bean, Italy's fava.

On the advice of a doctor, I had begun to take a quinine derivative to build up my resistance to malaria. Shortly thereafter, a brief episode of urinary bleeding sent me back to the same physician, who asked me many surprising questions. He wanted to know if I had any ancestors from the Mediterranean region. And, strangest of all, he asked if I had eaten fava beans recently.

Well, as it happened, I had, two days before at a Lebanese restaurant. I didn't think I had any Levantine forebears. But what was this all about? In addition to the various, more mundane problems the doctor was considering (quinine sensitivity, kidney stones), he had also thought to determine if I had a deficiency, common around the Mediterranean, of a blood enzyme called glucose-6-phosphate dehydrogenase (G6PD). If that was the case, it was just possible that either quinine or favas had touched off my bleeding. It turned out that I had plenty of G6PD, and my fleeting symptoms remained undiagnosed. While I have always regretted that I do not suffer from so recherché and elegant a malady as favism, I have decided that I am far happier to be able to indulge in favas unafraid. In our climate, roughly similar lima beans grow more easily. Favas like cool, moist conditions, such as they find in Europe, where their delicate flavor has made them a favorite since Homeric times. In a memorable, rustic simile from *The Iliad*, an arrow rebounding upward from the breastplate of Menelaus is compared to "dark-skinned favas and chickpeas" that "rise from a great threshing floor when struck by the winnower's fan." Theocritus, father of the pastoral, returned to the fava in his seventh idyll: "And on that day I will wreathe my brows . . . and draw the wine of Ptelea from the bowl as I lie by the fire, and someone will roast me favas in the fire."

By Theocritus's time, many authors had turned the fava and its Homeric companion the chickpea to literary account. Plato linked them together in *The Republic*. Xenophon, in a passage Theocritus evidently had in mind, wrote: "We must say such things while lying by the fire on a soft divan in winter season, being full, drinking sweet wine, munching chickpeas." Xenophon left out the favas; Theocritus put them back into his pastiche of Xenophon and left out the chickpeas. And underlying this learned bucolic play is a straightforward culinary fact. The ancients relished favas and chickpeas in their dried form. Today, a crazed fava hunger seizes Europeans in the spring, when the first favas come on the market, tender and green, edible raw from the pod.

On May Day in Rome, the greengrocers of the Campo dei Fiori sell picnickers piles of favas. Families trek off with their beans to simple restaurants for a *scampagnata fuoriporta*, a picnic outside the walls of the city. They order wine, shuck their favas, and eat them as is, or they may wrap them in slices of salami.

In England, the same madness possesses all classes of people. The season is somewhat later, but by the end of June, you will find "broad beans" holding pride of place on the tables of the most food-conscious British or artfully arrayed on dishes at that temple of cuisine the Auberge des Quatre-Saisons, in Great Milton between Oxford and London.

People with their own gardens, who have been nipping the tops of the shrubby broad bean plants since early spring to promote pod production and discourage aphids, can eat the freshest, youngest beans, pod and all, by simply boiling them in salted water for a few minutes until tender.

Gardeners and their friends are probably also the only people lucky enough to get broad beans that have not already developed tough skins around them. That saves them the trouble of skinning each bean.

Real broad bean fanatics, such as Richard Olney, the American author of *Simple French Food*, distinguish four separate stages of broad bean development, each one dictating a different culinary approach. Stage one, according to Olney, arrives when the peach-fuzzed pods are only 6 or 7 inches long and the skins don't have to be removed. At stage two, the pods have lengthened and flattened and swollen around the beans. The skins are green but tough and have to be popped off after the briefest blanching. Then, the tender naked beans take only a couple of minutes to cook. Olney throws in a sprig of savory, the classic French accompaniment for broad beans. He, like most of us, has not been persuaded by Elizabeth David that savory spoils the flavor of the beans with its own peppery bitterness.

Stages three and four involve favas too mature to bother with. Unless you grow favas yourself, you will probably never see these bigger, mealier beans, which are normally dried.

7 pounds fava beans in their pods

Olive oil for cooking

¼ pound cured, unsmoked bacon, preferably from the jowl (you may find this
   at Italian butchers or delicatessens, but regular unsmoked bacon, pancetta, will
   substitute nicely, as will Spanish ham—*jamón serrano*).

½ onion, peeled and chopped

Salt

Pepper

1. Shell the beans. If they are very young and green, proceed to step 2. Otherwise, boil the shelled beans, uncovered, in lightly salted water for 2 minutes, drain, cool, and pop off the outer skins. If you have time, refrigerate the beans in a plastic bag for a few hours after boiling to firm them up so that the skinning will be less likely to damage them.

2. Heat the oil in a skillet. Cut away any rind from the bacon and dice. Sauté in the hot oil with the onion until the onion is translucent. Add the favas and the salt and pepper. Toss together with the bacon and onion until the beans are heated through, about 2 minutes. Serve right away.

Serves 8 to 10

pasta e fagioli alla pordenonense
noodles and beans in the style of pordenone

Aside from spaghetti, this was the first Italian dish I ever heard about. It was a big joke, or supposed to be. TV comics of the early fifties assumed they could always get a laugh by bringing up *pasta fazool*, a dialectal version of *pasta e fagioli* (pasta and beans). I didn't get the joke as a child, and I don't want to get it now. Of course, now nobody would dream of trying to get a yuck from saying something in peasant Italian, unless it was somehow connected to the Mob. Too many people still think organized crime and its alleged folkways are hilarious.

On an episode of *The Sopranos*, the mafiosi wives go to a lecture at their church in New Jersey to hear an advanced Italian-American woman give them a pep talk on how they'd all come a long way, baby. One of the speaker's self-esteem–building examples was gastronomic: "When they [people making fun of your lifestyle] say spaghetti and meatballs, you say eggplant parmigiana and broccoli rabe." It gets worse: "When they say your mothers wore black, you say we wear Armani."

The wives are furious. They think this woman is putting them down, that she is agreeing with the Italian-hating world that there is something embarrassing or low class about unreconstructed Sicilian-American food or other features of the world their immigrant ancestors created in America. I don't get it, because I don't believe that one recipe is classier than another—more complex, more expensive, sure, but intrinsically superior, not on your life.

The truth is that pasta fazool is a pan-Italian dish with many variations on the same idea: noodles cooked together with beans, starch on starch. There are four basic varieties of this dish: with lard, with olive oil, pureed, and not pureed. In all of these categories, the beans are cooked until quite soft.

This opulent recipe from Pordenone, in the Friuli region of the extreme northeast of Italy, goes beyond the basic idea of the dish, adding potatoes, which are unusual for Italy but typical up there. I have tried pasta e fagioli with lard and prefer it that way. I am also amused by the belt-and-suspenders inclusion of unpureed beans with the puree.

When you serve it, if a guest, suppressing a giggle, says pasta fazool, you say— Actually, better not.

Salt

1½ pounds dried cranberry beans (borlotti), soaked in cold water for 24 hours

1 medium onion, peeled and studded with 3 peeled garlic cloves

1 small celery stalk, chopped

4 potatoes, peeled and diced

1 bay leaf

3 pig's feet, or 1 small hambone with some meat on it, or 3 spareribs

¼ pound pasta, ditalini or tagliatelle

Olive oil

1. Bring 4 quarts of water to the boil. Add salt and all the other ingredients except the pasta and the olive oil.

2. Simmer for 3 hours. Set aside about a third of the beans.

3. Remove the pork and discard the bones. Remove all the other solid ingredients (discarding the bay leaf) from the cooking liquid with a slotted spoon and run them through a food mill with the meat.

4. Return the pureed mixture and the reserved whole beans to the original cooking liquid. Bring to a boil, add the pasta, and cook until tender, about 10 minutes: Al dente texture is not desirable for this dish.

5. Remove from the heat and let stand for 10 minutes. Just before serving, stir in a soupspoon of olive oil.

Serves 6

puree-mousse of green beans à la michel guérard

Michel Guérard, the outstanding culinary intelligence of the nouvelle cuisine in France in the early 1970s, got tagged as a cook for dieters because his book *Cuisine Minceur* became a best seller. He also opened a gourmet health spa in southwest France. But his real contribution was as a chef with grand and original ideas not intended to make anyone thin. I ate in his original restaurant in a gritty suburb of Paris, Le Pot-au-Feu at Asnières, during Holy Week of 1972. It was a revelation, radical and delicious. *That* Guérard wrote *La Cuisine Gourmande* (1978). Among other glories, it contains his recipes for those vegetable puree-mousses he invented and served hot with main courses—beets (see page 32), celery, leeks, and green beans, all paragons of the simple elegance that originally carried the day for nouvelle cuisine.

1 pound green beans, topped and tailed
Salt
2 tablespoons crème fraîche
2 tablespoons butter
Pepper

1. Cook the beans for 10 minutes, uncovered, in 6 cups of lightly salted, vigorously boiling water. Drain and "refresh" in cold water. Drain again.

2. Puree in a blender. Add the crème fraiche to the puree in the blender. Puree for another minute. Scrape into a serving dish.

3. Melt the butter in a small skillet. Continue over medium heat until the foam subsides and the butter turns light brown. Pour over the beans, add pepper to taste, and mix in with a whisk. Serve while still hot or keep hot in a bain-marie or double boiler until ready to serve.

Serves 4

sichuan dry-fried green beans
gan bian si ji dou

This simple but time-consuming dish is a classic of the cuisine of Sichuan, but it is not torridly seasoned with chilies or Sichuan peppercorns. This does not make it atypical. In fact it illustrates one of the fifty-six cooking methods of the Sichuanese canon listed in the standard Sichuan culinary encyclopedia and quoted in full in Fuchsia Dunlop's *Land of Plenty* (2001), itself now the standard work on the subject in English. *Gan bian*, explains Ms. Dunlop, involves "food cut into slivers or strips . . . stirred constantly in a wok with very little oil, over a medium flame, until it is slightly dried out and beautifully fragrant." The other version of gan bian si ji dou that I have seen, in *Mrs. Chiang's Szechwan Cookbook* by Ellen Schrecker (1976), adds soaked dried shrimp instead of ground pork to the beans. There are other small differences, but both recipes include Sichuan pickled vegetable, or *ya cai*, a quite salty preserved root of turnip. The long-cooked beans give the dish its crucial texture; the ya cai its distinctive flavor.

Ms. Dunlop notes that restaurants often deep-fry the beans to speed up the cooking. You are free to disapprove once you have done the dish the traditional way.

6 tablespoons any flavorless cooking oil

1 pound green beans, topped, tailed, and cut into 2-inch pieces

¼ pound ground pork or ½ cup dried shrimp, soaked for 2 hours in hot water, then finely chopped

1 tablespoon rice wine for cooking

1 tablespoon soy sauce

3 tablespoons ya cai (Sichuan pickled vegetable), finely chopped

1½ teaspoons sesame oil

1. Heat 3 tablespoons of the cooking oil in a wok until the oil smokes. Lower the heat to medium. Add the beans all at once and stir-fry until they are tender, 6 to 10 minutes. Drain and discard any remaining oil. Set the beans aside.

2. Heat the remaining 3 tablespoons oil in the wok until it just begins to smoke. Add the pork or the chopped dried shrimp and stir-fry for about 30 seconds. Along the way, add the rice wine and soy sauce.

3. Add the ya cai and stir briefly. Then return the beans to the wok. Stir until hot. Remove to a serving dish. Stir in the sesame oil and serve.

Serves 6 as a side dish or one of several dishes in a Chinese-style meal

succotash

Here is a real Native American dish. Narragansett Indians legendarily taught settlers to mix corn and beans, a dish they called *msickquatash* (boiled corn kernels). It quickly passed into the mainstream American menu and then into folklore. Now best known from Daffy Duck's exasperated outcry, "Sufferin' Succotash," this is a drastically underrated heirloom, when the ingredients are treated with respect.

⅓ cup corn oil
2 cups fresh or defrosted frozen corn kernels
2 cups fresh or defrosted frozen baby limas
Salt

1. Heat the oil in a cast-iron skillet until a pinch of bread tossed in it sizzles.
2. Stir in the corn and beans. Keep stirring to mix them together. Remove from the heat as soon as the beans have brightened in color and softened just enough to chew easily. If you let them go longer, you will be reminded of pasty lima beans at school.
3. Toss in salt and serve.

Variations: Steam over simmering water in a couscousière or Chinese steamer for a fat-free dish. For a fat-rich dish, toss with 4 rashers of crumbled bacon or ½ cup of chicken skin and cracklings, browned in chicken fat and roughly chopped.

Serves 6 as a side dish or 3 as a main course

beets

Beta vulgaris is not a fancy plant. You can, if you insist, buy modern cultivars that aren't red. But I think that yellow or white beets are freakish. And don't start with me about the virtues of the striped Chioggia beet. This sport of nature is a slur on a perfectly decent town on the Adriatic near Venice. It is true that Chioggia's original Latin name, Clodia Fossa, means the ditch of Clodius, after the Trojan refugee who founded it, and that it has never quite recovered from the Chioggian War (1379–1380) when it got caught between the armies of Venice and Genoa. But Chioggia is a pretty place, as well as the hometown of the great rococo portraitist Rosalba Carriera (1675–1757), and deserves better than to be remembered mainly for a beet that resembles a Swiss Guard.

Real beets are red, or have been since the

seventeenth century. Their color, a combination of purple betacyanin and yellow betaxanthin, is not fast. It runs and drips, and will stain counters and clothes and your urine. High in sugar but bolstered by a touch of acid, beets are delicious, cheap, versatile, and easy to cook.

Boil them in salted water for around 40 minutes, depending on size, until a fork goes in easily. Cool in cold water and squeeze off the skins. Before you cook beets, trim off the spinachlike greens, leaving an inch of stem. If the greens look nice, rinse and steam them, like spinach. For complete beet refinement, cut away the stems and sauté them separately.

The lazy way to cook beets may actually enhance their taste more than boiling. Just bake them for around 40 minutes in a 375-degree oven in a lightly moistened pan covered with aluminum foil. Some people eat beets raw, sliced or chopped into salad.

beet mousse

Michel Guérard, chef de file of the nouvelle cuisine of the seventies, invented a whole mini-cuisine of vegetable mousses (see also mousse of green beans, page 27). To my mind, they are among the most typical and most lastingly successful of the recipes created by a revolutionary culinary movement that reexamined and recombined classic ideas without, in its better moments, ever losing sight of the fundamental taste and character of ingredients. This is an adaptation of Guérard's recipe in *Cuisine Gourmande* (1978).

1 tomato

2 tablespoons oil

1 large onion, peeled and sliced thin

1 garlic clove, smashed and peeled

¼ cup red wine vinegar

¾ pound beets, peeled, trimmed, and sliced thin

Salt

Pepper

1 tablespoon heavy cream, approximately

½ cup chicken stock, approximately

1. Bring 6 cups of water to a boil. Immerse the tomato and count to 10. Remove the tomato with a slotted spoon and run it under cold water to stop the cooking. With a small sharp knife, pull away the skin. Put the tomato in a colander. Press lightly on it with a wooden spoon so that its liquid flows away. Remove and discard the seeds. Chop roughly and reserve.

2. Heat the oil in a skillet. Reduce the heat and simmer the onion and garlic until the onion is translucent. Pour in the vinegar and deglaze the pan with a metal spatula. Add the reserved tomato and the beet slices. Season with salt and pepper. Cover and simmer gently for 1 hour over low-medium heat.

3. Transfer the contents of the skillet into a processor fitted with the steel blade. Process for 2 to 3 minutes. Scrape into a saucepan. Whisk in the heavy cream and the chicken stock. Add more if necessary to produce a smooth, light puree. Serve hot.

Serves 4 as an accompaniment to a main course of red meat or chicken

greek cold beet and garlic puree

As with almost all Greek dishes, there is probably a Turkish precursor of this simple but masterful combination of two humble ingredients. But I encountered it first in a Times Square Greek restaurant of no pretension but immense professionalism. You don't have to be Greek—or Turkish—to slap this together while studying Greek irregular verbs or working on your abs. It keeps for several days in the refrigerator, but put the two ingredients together at the last minute to avoid having the snow-white garlic turning pink from beet-juice runoff.

2 pounds beets, trimmed
2 heads garlic

1. Boil the beets in enough water to cover them amply. Do not cover the pan. Test after a half hour. Remove any beets that are pierced easily with a fork. The smaller ones will cook faster than the larger ones. When they have all cooked and have cooled enough to handle, push away the outer skin with your fingers and press out the stem.

2. Slice the beets about ¼ inch thick. Arrange the pieces on a serving plate in an overlapping line, two lines or a circle, from smallest to largest. Decorate with beet greens.

3. Separate the cloves from the garlic heads. Smash them with a knife. Remove the skins and discard. Pound the garlic cloves to a homogeneous mash with a mortar and pestle, or chop them roughly with a large knife. Arrange in a mound with the beet slices. Serve at room temperature.

Serves 6 as a first course

harvard beets

I don't think I ate Harvard beets at Harvard, but I was glad to learn, in a recent number of the *Harvard University Gazette*, that Associate Professor of Psychiatry William A. Carlezon, Jr.'s research has shown that beets can mitigate depression—in rats. Beets contain uridine, a nucleoside that seems to make rodents lively but leaves them indolent when they are deprived of it. Whether this works on humans is not for me to say, but where is the harm in downing beets when you feel blue? Harvard beets are clearly not harmful, but they are a bit gloppy. If this has kept you off them, just leave out the cornstarch. That will also eliminate the mirrorlike sheen of the traditional sauce but will not affect the sweet-and-sour flavor that defines the dish.

8 medium trimmed beets

1 cup red wine vinegar

1 cup sugar

1 tablespoon cornstarch (optional)

3 cloves

Salt

2 tablespoons butter

1. Boil the beets until fork-tender, about 30 minutes or possibly more if they are large or old. Let cool, peel, and slice.

2. Combine the remaining ingredients (cornstarch optional) in a 6-cup saucepan. Simmer for 3 to 4 minutes, stirring. Add the beets. Continue simmering until the beets are heated through and the sauce has taken on their color. Remove the cloves and serve.

Serves 8

russian beet borscht

If you think, and why shouldn't you, that borscht is a plain Russian beet soup, lightly soured with lemon juice and topped with a dollop of sour cream, you would be astonished to see how many variations there are on this homely theme in Russian cookbooks. Beets are the only common thread, which makes sense if you know that "borscht" descends from a word in the Russian language's predecessor, Old Church Slavonic. Now, in Russian, "borscht" refers only to the soup (or soups) with beets in them (the modern Russian word for beet is etymologically unrelated to "borscht." It means cow parsnip, a member of the carrot family [*Heracleum maximum*] whose parsniplike root was evidently the original ingredient of the soup).

My friend Anne Volokh, now a *grande dame* in Los Angeles, was once a food writer for the Sunday edition of the Soviet newspaper *Izvestia*. After emigrating from the U.S.S.R., she published the definitive Russian cookbook in English, *The Art of Russian Cuisine* (1983), in which she recollects a culinary idyll she spent by herself as a teenager in a rented cottage in the Ukrainian countryside (she was born in Kiev) cooking the primordial borscht, the Ukrainian variety:

> *My peasant neighbors proved to be sympathetic and readily supplied me with beets, carrots, cabbage and new potatoes, cucumbers and tomatoes, parsley and dill from their vegetable gardens, and wonderful fresh pot cheese and sour cream from their kitchens.*

Ms. Volokh's Ukrainian borscht, recollected in prosperous exile in California, includes among other extras: spareribs, ham, white beans, mushrooms, garlic, and tomato paste. She tells us of special borscht dumplings, too, and an even richer version of the soup that substitutes duck or goose for the humbler meats.

There are many more borschts (which should really be spelled borshch, as in Khrushchev, reflecting the Russian consonant, a single letter, that the Russian aviatrix in George Bernard Shaw's *Misalliance* explains should be pronounced like fishchurch) in the Soviet-era *Ukrainian Cuisine*, published in Kiev in an English edition in 1975. Twenty-five to be exact. Among them: borscht with carp, with meatballs, with mushrooms and prunes, with eggplant, with buckwheat pastry "ears," and with beans. In other sources, you can find still others, the most distinctive including either *rossl*, the fermented beet liquid, or *kvas*, a beer made from bread.

The prepared, bottled borscht sold in almost every U.S. supermarket is the streamlined preparation that Ms. Volokh calls cold beet soup (although hers has hard-boiled eggs). For me, this is the classic, the unembellished Platonic version, and also the one that has escaped from Russia and its pogroms and purges, brought by Jewish refugees to join the wide world as a universal dish.

2 dozen medium beets with their greens
1 tablespoon lemon juice
Salt
½ teaspoon sugar
Sour cream
Snipped dill leaves

1. Cut off the beet greens and wash thoroughly. Chop into 2-inch lengths. Peel and slice the beets.
2. Bring 6 cups of water to a boil. Add the beets and greens. Stir in the lemon juice, salt to taste, and the sugar. Simmer for 20 minutes, or until the beets are tender but not mushy.
3. Remove the greens and reserve for use as a vegetable. Let the soup cool completely, and then chill.
4. Serve well chilled. Pass the sour cream and dill separately.

Serves 10

black-eyed peas

*V*igna inguiculata is a bean, not a pea, of African origin, brought by slaves across the Atlantic and a feature of post–slave food from northeast Brazil to the Carolinas. Its pealike seeds can be eaten whole or milled as flour. In some places in the U.S. South, black-eyed peas are called cowpeas or field peas.

acarajes
brazilian black-eyed-pea fritters

You can use either a charcoal brazier or an electric hot plate to fry acarajes, but it's better to do it outdoors. Palm oil, when heated, gives off a strong odor. That's why Bahians call it *azeite-de-cheiro*, "odorous oil," and that's also why it's advisable to heat the oil outside. Do not serve acaraje as a formal dish at lunch or dinner. That would be inconceivable. It should be served as an hors d'oeuvre or appetizer before the meal. Acaraje goes well with a *meladinha* (rum flavored with honey and anise) or *batida de limao* (lemonade).

The traditional accompaniment is acaraje sauce, a mixture of dried malagueta pepper (a noncapsicum pepper originally from West Africa, but available from Brazilian specialty sources), shelled dried shrimp, chopped onion, and salt—all fried in palm oil until chestnut brown. Almost any other hot sauce will suffice.

For an authentic presentation, line a wicker basket with a banana leaf, and put the acarajes on top while they're still hot. If you don't have banana leaves, give the guests paper napkins before serving the acarajes. No plates or silverware. Just hands.

Keep another basket handy—like the one with the acarajes in it—for the used banana leaves or paper napkins.

"Open" the acarajes by cutting a slit in them to put in the sauce just before serving. If somebody doesn't want to eat the sauce, leave her acaraje whole; don't open it.

(This recipe derives from *Caderno de Comidas Baianas*, by Joaquim da Costa Pinto Netto, Tempo Brasileiro, 1986; with thanks to Hélio Gáspari.)

2 cups (about 1 pound) black-eyed peas
2 medium onions, peeled
Salt
Palm oil for deep-frying

1. Let the black-eyed peas soak in water for 24 or even 36 hours. After that time, you can rub away the skins from the peas with your fingers. In this way, the "black eyes" will come off. Once they're skinned, put the peas through a meat grinder fitted with the finest of its perforated disks. This will produce a uniform dough.

2. Grate one of the onions or put it through the meat grinder and add it to the bean dough. Add salt to taste.

3. Beat the dough well with a wooden spoon. Do not use an electric mixer for this process. It would make the dough too fine. The essential thing is that the ingredients

should be well mixed. Also, don't let the dough get too stiff, or if it does, add a little cold water.

4. Put plenty of palm oil in a deep-frying kettle. Add the remaining onion, whole, to the oil and set over high heat. When the oil begins to smoke lightly, it's time to begin frying the acaraje.

5. With a wooden spoon, spoon out some dough and let it slip into the hot oil without immersing the spoon. The ball of dough should float in the oil; with another wooden spoon, turn the acaraje so that it fries on all sides. Don't let the fritters fry so long that they get too dark. An acaraje should end up looking like a beautiful sunset in Bahia.

Makes 6 acarajes

hoppin' john

This stew of rice, black-eyed peas, and rendered pork is a traditional New Year's Day dish in Charleston, S.C., where it was supposedly once hawked on the street by a one-legged black man named John.

2 cups (about 1 pound) dried black-eyed peas

½ pound salt pork, bacon, or smoked hog jowl, sliced

Hot sauce

Salt

2 tablespoons bacon fat or lard

2 medium onions, peeled and finely chopped

1 cup raw long-grain rice

1. Soak the peas overnight in 6 cups of cold water.

2. Bring the soaked peas and their water to a boil, add the pork, hot sauce, and salt to taste, reduce the heat, and simmer until the peas are tender, around 20 minutes. Drain and reserve the solid ingredients.

3. While the peas cook, heat the bacon fat or lard and sauté the onions in it until soft. Meanwhile, bring 1½ cups of water to a boil.

4. Add the boiling water and the onions with their cooking fat to the peas and pork in a large saucepan. Stir in the rice, cover, and cook over medium heat until the rice is cooked and the water is absorbed.

Serves 8

bok choy

feel about bok choy as Supreme Court Justice Potter Stewart did about obscenity. It is hard to define, but I know it when I see it. More serious foragers in Chinese markets allow themselves to get bogged down in the not insignificant differences separating bok choy or pak choi from Canton, Shanghai, Taiwan (or Fengshan); choy sum, tatsoi, and yau choy, in their seedling, baby, mature, and flowering varieties, not to mention white-stemmed, dwarf-stemmed, and green-stemmed forms, some of which are different stages or different names for each other. The scientific name is even less help, especially when dealing with Chinese greengrocers, who know no more than you do about the fine taxonomic nuances of *Brassica rapa*, Chinensis group. Nor does it reduce the nomenclatural turbidity to know that the English vernacular names for this group of Brassica—among them Chinese cabbage, Chinese celery cabbage, Chinese white cabbage—may easily be confused with that other Chinese cabbage of the same species, *B. rapa*, Pekinensis group, the cabbagey white, leafy plant also known as Napa, *da bai cai, wong bok*, and—*horribile dictu*—bok choy. Then there is the matter of Chinese broccoli or kale, *B. oleracea*, Alboglabra group, which I am going to ignore in order to achieve what St. Paul called the peace "which passeth all understanding."*

Suffice it to say that in the real world of vegetable markets in the West, it is almost impossible to confuse the two great groups of Chinese cabbages. The large stalkless white cabbagey types are Pekinensis and will be sold either as Napa or simply Chinese cabbage. The green-leafed plants with the stalks are the Chinensis group, and almost anyone, even a botanist, is likely to call them "bok choy" when speaking English. For my taste, the type that most merits a trip to Chinatown is any small bok choy variety with the tiny flowers. Tender and succulent, this variety, like all the others of its group, is normally stir-fried. The cook triumphs over Nature in all her perplexing diversity.

*Philippians 4:7

sichuan-style stir-fried bok choy

2 pounds bok choy

3 tablespoons peanut oil

4 slices peeled ginger

2 garlic cloves, peeled

Salt

½ teaspoon sugar

1 tablespoon sesame oil

8 dried red chiles

2 teaspoons whole Sichuan peppercorns

Chinkiang or black vinegar (optional)

1. Cut the stem ends off the bok choy. Then cut the stalks into 1-inch sections.

2. Heat the wok, then add the peanut oil and heat over a medium flame until very hot but not smoking.

3. For a generic stir-fry of bok choy, toss in the ginger and stir-fry for a few seconds. Then stir in the bok choy and garlic. Continue stir-frying for 2 minutes, or until the bok choy has lost its turgor but the leaves are still bright green. Season with salt, sugar, and sesame oil.

4. For a Sichuanese quick-fry (*qiang*) of bok choy, substitute the chiles and Sichuan peppercorns for the ginger and garlic. Add both ingredients as soon as the oil is hot and stir-fry very briefly. Then add the bok choy sections and proceed as above. Fuchsia Dunlop recommends adding a splash of black vinegar just before serving "for a fabulous extra kick of flavor."

Serves 4

broccoli

Let's raise the flag for broccoli, a harmless plant in troubled times. *Brassica oleracea*, Cymosa group, is easy to identify in the market, but botanically almost indistinguishable from cauliflower. Common sense suggests that it was first cultivated in Italy as a hybrid of cauliflower some time in the modern period, since references to it do not appear in writing before the eighteenth century. The flowerets can be eaten raw and dipped in mayonnaise, as they are at thousands of cocktail receptions every year, offering a green contrast to the cauliflowerets on the same buffet. At the dinner table, they mostly appear steamed, with hollandaise sauce if the cook is ambitious. Soup is the way to go if the great broccolophobic Bush the first is coming to dinner. The other guests will love it, too, and the ex-president won't know what he's eating.

puree of broccoli soup   45

puree of broccoli soup

1 pound broccoli
4 tablespoons butter
3 cups chicken stock
½ cup heavy cream
Salt

1. Cut off the tips of the broccoli stalks and discard. Then cut the stalks from the flowerets. Set aside a handful of the flowerets. Peel the stalks with a vegetable peeler and then slice the stalks into ¼-inch rounds.

2. Melt the butter in a medium skillet over medium heat. When the foam subsides, stir in the sliced stalks, cover, and let simmer until the stalk slices have softened. Add the flowerets (except the reserved handful) and sauté, uncovered, with the stalks until they have softened.

3. Process the cooked broccoli. Then force the puree through a food mill or other medium strainer into a clean saucepan. Stir in the chicken stock and the heavy cream, and salt to taste. Serve chilled or hot. Either way, toss in the reserved flowerets at the last minute.

Serves 4

brussels sprouts

B russels sprouts
(*Brassica oleracea*, Gemmifera group) did in
fact originate in Belgium as a mutant or
dwarf cultivar of Savoy cabbage. It surfaced
in the sixteenth century and spread to the
U.S. only after 1800, but never captured the
hearts and minds of the people. Indeed,
before I learned the historical truth, my
assumption was that the plant's name was
intended as a slur, part of a widespread
humorous tradition of anti-Belgian
invective. This tradition, the moral
equivalent of Polish jokes in the U.S. and
Aggie jokes in Texas, eventually became a
joke on its own, so that in France the
expression *"c'est Belge"* evolved as a
humorous play on the normal phrase *"c'est
bète,"* or that's dumb. Mark Twain, ever
ready to lampoon a *Brassica* (see under

cauliflower, page 70), once said that to eat Brussels sprouts was to deprive cabbage of their young.

Despite all this, Brussels sprouts appear on supermarket shelves all year, and somebody must be eating them. The standard method is to trim away tough or withered leaves, cut an *X* at the stem end to promote even cooking, and boil in salted water until tender. For a far grander presentation try this molded loaf.

pain de choux de bruxelles
brussels sprouts loaf

Salt

2¼ pounds Brussels sprouts

8 tablespoons butter

Pepper

½ teaspoon ground nutmeg

2 cups milk

½ cup dried bread crumbs

2 egg yolks, lightly beaten

2 tablespoons flour

3 parsley sprigs

⅓ cup heavy cream

1. Bring 6 quarts of water containing 3 tablespoons salt to a boil. While you wait, slice off just enough of the stem ends of the Brussels sprouts so that the leaves remain attached to each other. When the water comes to a full rolling boil, add the Brussels sprouts and cook, uncovered, for 10 minutes, or until the Brussels sprouts are barely fork-tender. Drain in a colander and let cool.

2. Handful by handful, squeeze as much water as you can out of the Brussels sprouts. Process in small batches and transfer to a saucepan. Add 6 tablespoons butter, salt and pepper to taste, and ¼ teaspoon ground nutmeg. Set over very low heat and stir with a wooden spoon until the butter melts.

3. Heat ½ cup milk in a small saucepan until it starts to foam. Remove from the heat and stir in the bread crumbs. Let stand for 10 minutes. Then pour into a strainer and press gently with a wooden spoon to extract the excess liquid. Stir the moistened bread crumbs into the Brussels sprouts mixture along with the egg yolks.

4. Preheat the oven to 350 degrees. Bring 4 cups of water to a boil in a teakettle. Use 1 tablespoon butter to grease the inside of a 6-cup charlotte or soufflé mold.

5. Scrape the Brussels sprouts mixture into the greased mold. Set the mold inside a larger, higher-walled saucepan. Pour the boiling water into the space between the mold and the inside of the saucepan, to a height of 2 inches. Set this assemblage gently onto a rack about one third up from the bottom of the oven. Cover the saucepan (not the mold). This allows warm, moist air to circulate gently over the top of the "loaf" and prevents a crust from forming. After 5 minutes, lower the oven temperature to 325 degrees and bake for another 55 minutes. From time to time check that the water

is not quite boiling. If it is boiling, remove a bit with a baster and replace with some cold water.

6. Meanwhile, prepare a cream sauce. First make a blond roux by heating the remaining tablespoon of butter with the flour over low heat in a 6-cup saucepan, working it into a homogeneous paste with a wooden spoon for a few minutes, just enough so that the roux loses any raw flour taste but does not color. Remove from the heat. Bring the remaining 1½ cups milk to a boil and whisk into the roux. Whisk in the parsley as well as salt, pepper, and ground nutmeg to taste. Simmer for 10 minutes. Remove the parsley and discard. Keep whisking until the boiling sauce reduces by half, to about ¾ cup. Reduce the heat as the sauce thickens. It should be quite thick. Finally, over very low heat, whisk in the heavy cream. Reduce, if necessary, to achieve the thickness you desire. Keep warm until ready to serve.

7. Test the "loaf" by piercing it with a trussing needle. The needle should come out clean. Run a knife around the perimeter of the loaf. Then invert a serving plate of appropriate size over the top of the mold. With one hand on the plate and the other on the bottom of the mold, invert the mold and set the mold and platter on the counter, platter down. Lift the mold. The loaf should slide out in one piece.

8. Serve right away. Strain the sauce through a chinois into a sauceboat and pass separately.

Serves 6

cabbage

Cabbage (*Brassica oleracea*) is the ancestor of Brussels sprouts as well as cauliflower, broccoli, kale, and kohlrabi—all of which belong to the same species. The *Brassica* genus also includes Chinese cabbage, Chinese kale, some mustards and mustard greens, rape (the source of Canola oil), turnips, and rutabaga.

Cabbage has been around for a long time, at least as long as Egyptian hieroglyphics; so people have had ample opportunity to devise toothsome ways to prepare it. For some of us, it has worn out its welcome. A well-bred Radcliffe bluestocking once fled my house as soon as she sniffed cabbage steaming in the kitchen. Cabbage does emit a strong odor, but I think the young woman's antipathy was based more on unhappy memories of overcooked cabbage than on the aroma itself. I like the smell because it portends a delightfully flavored, just-short-of-mushy wedge flavored with salt, caraway, butter, and a little red wine.

Sauerkraut is the preeminent cabbage preparation. It is almost always a side dish, as in the vile sauerkraut served with dreary hot dogs from rolling carts all over Manhattan. This is a degraded version of sauerkraut's acme, the French *choucroute*, a porky fantasia in which sauerkraut plays a major part. An equally sublime first cousin of choucroute is *podvarak*, a Serbian symbiosis of sauerkraut, fowl, and cayenne pepper.

I am also including tuned-up versions of cabbage recipes from my childhood and perhaps yours: coleslaw and stuffed cabbage. This is not the place for haute cuisine "turned" cabbages, those tiny "heads" reassembled from parcooked cabbages and served as part of the garniture on the elaborately composed platters of the heyday of *service à la russe*.

choucroute

The name basically means cabbage chomp. The best ones I ever had were made in restaurants in Strasbourg, capital of Alsace, the Rhenish eastern frontier of France where what must have been a German idea got purified in francophone kitchens, whose twin gods are Gargantua and Descartes. Aficionados may argue about which meats should be included in an *echt* choucroute, but no one disputes that the real point of all that pork is to glorify the sauerkraut.

3 pounds sauerkraut

½ pound fat (lard, goose fat, duck fat, or other meat drippings)

10 juniper berries

2 cups white wine

½ pound bacon (and/or kielbasa, or cocktail franks)

1 pound salt pork (belly, hock, ear, or jowl), soaked in a large amount of cold water for 2 hours

1½ pounds ham in a single piece

6 smoked pig's knuckles

1. Rinse the sauerkraut thoroughly to remove all traces of the brine in which it was cured. Soak for 15 minutes. Rinse several times in a colander until the water comes out clear. Take the rinsed sauerkraut, a handful at a time, and squeeze out as much residual moisture as you can. Then leave to drain further in a colander set over a bowl.

2. Preheat the oven to 350 degrees.

3. Put the sauerkraut in a Dutch oven and cover with cold water. Add the fat, the juniper berries tied up in a piece of cloth, and the white wine. Cover the sauerkraut mixture with a greased circle of wax paper cut to fill the inside of the pot. Put on the lid and set in the oven.

4. After 3 hours, remove and discard the wax paper; add the bacon and the other meats, mixing them into the sauerkraut and covering them with it. Continue the oven, braising for 2 hours to completely cook the sauerkraut, which should completely absorb the liquid by the end. Pay close attention to the two converging processes—the doneness of the cabbage and the imbibition of the liquid—toward the end of the 5 hours. If the absorption of the liquid occurs too quickly, add more liquid—half water, half wine—a glass at a time, as needed.

5. To serve, separate the sauerkraut and the meats. Slice the meats, where appropriate, and put a selection of them on each plate with some sauerkraut.

Serves 6 to 8

coleslaw

As Alan Davidson notes in *The Oxford Companion to Food*, coleslaw is a Dutch dish, appropriated from New Amsterdam settlers by non-Dutch Americans who distorted *koolsla* (Dutch for cabbage salad) into the confusing but now universal side dish. If made with real mayonnaise and cut nicely, coleslaw rises above the ruck of wan versions served in pleated paper cuplets at fast-food restaurants and in delis. Caraway seeds can be added for a touch of anise flavor. Try slicing in a hot banana pepper for an eye-opening variation.

1 large head cabbage

1 large carrot, scraped

1 medium onion, peeled

1 egg yolk

⅓ cup vinegar

1 tablespoon mustard

1 cup corn or other non-olive oil

Salt

White pepper

1. Discard the outer leaves of the cabbage. Cut the cabbage into quarters. Remove and discard the core.
2. Cut the cabbage quarters into smaller pieces that can be put through the julienne blade of the processor. Julienne the carrot and the onion.
3. Mix together the ingredients from step 2 in a large serving bowl.
4. In a small bowl, whisk together the egg yolk, the vinegar, and the mustard. Then dribble in the oil, whisking vigorously as you go. Add only a little at first, whisking until the sauce "takes." Then add a little more. After a bit you can increase the additions of oil until you have used it all up. It should be fairly thick.
5. Add salt and pepper to taste. Then toss with the cabbage and serve.

Serves 6 to 8 as a side dish or salad

podvarak

I first tasted this in Pittsburgh at a political hangout called Sarah's, in an old town-house miraculously surviving in the shadow of the dark Satanic steel mills. Later, I made some myself, in the summer, on a sultry night when the motionless air and the very high seasoning made us sweat like the pigs we'd been. I had a deadline to meet for an article on cabbage. You should wait until December to make this surprising dish.

1 cup lard
3 large onions, peeled and chopped
2 tablespoons cayenne
1 tablespoon salt
5 pounds sauerkraut, drained and thoroughly rinsed
One 8- to 10-pound goose

1. Melt the lard in a heavy skillet and stir in the onions. Sauté over medium heat until soft and lightly browned. Remove from the heat.

2. Preheat the oven to 350 degrees.

3. In a large roasting pan, stir together the onion-lard mixture with the cayenne, the salt, and the sauerkraut. Wring out any excess water from the sauerkraut before you add it.

4. Spread the onion-sauerkraut mixture over the bottom of the roasting pan. Set the goose on top of it, breast down. Prick the skin all over with a fork. Put in the oven and roast for about 2 hours, basting frequently. If the sauerkraut begins to stick to the pan, add a cup of water.

5. Carve the goose. Transfer the sauerkraut mixture to a serving bowl and pass separately.

Serves 6 to 8

stuffed cabbage

As a favor to a gardener friend in Montecito, Calif., I agreed to give a speech at a dinner meeting of the national flower-show judges of the Garden Clubs of America, held under the glorious Tiffany skylight of the main dining room of that pinnacle of well-born New York femininity, The Colony Club. Since the only plants I know much about are grown for the table, and lecturing to flower ladies about edible blooms seemed a bit like giving a speech on infanticide to obstetricians, I was stumped about picking a subject.* To the rescue came Patti Hagan, then gardening columnist for my page at the *Wall Street Journal* and a horticultural activist. "Tell them about leaves used for wrapping food," she said.

So I told them about leaves used for wrapping food, about stuffed grape leaves and tamales (corn husk–wrapped and avocado leaf–wrapped) and a great many others, which the assembled judges purported to judge completely fascinating. First among these intrafoliate dishes was, of course, stuffed cabbage.

Like the wheel, this ingenious dodge for enclosing food in a protective, edible, nonpastry container was invented in many places by many cultures that had access to cheap cabbage and ovens. There are basically two ways to proceed: Stuff individual leaves or as below, leave the head intact, smear the *farce* on the leaves and then tie up the treated cabbage so that it looks as if nothing had happened to it.

1 medium (2½-pound) green cabbage

9 ounces ground beef, veal, or pork, about 1 cup

2 ounces salt pork or fatback, diced, about ¼ cup

1 tablespoon salt

1 tablespoon finely chopped parsley

¼ cup dry white wine

2 sheets of salt pork or fatback to wrap the cabbage

1 medium onion, peeled and sliced

1 carrot, scraped and cut into rounds

3 cups beef stock, approximately

1. Trim the stalk end of the cabbage so that the cabbage will sit level. Remove any tough or discolored outer leaves and discard. With a small sharp knife, cut out as much of the solid core of the cabbage without detaching any leaves. This permits the cooking liquid to reach the inside of the cabbage more efficiently, and keeps the cabbage from floating. Discard the core.

*Even the word "picking" had taken on a controversial flavor, so to speak.

2. Put the cabbage in a pot to blanch and cover it with cold water. Cover the pot and set it over high heat. It should take about 45 minutes for the water to boil. As soon as this happens, remove the cabbage gently and drain in a colander.

3. While the cabbage blanches, process the ground meat, salt pork, salt, and parsley together. Use the steel blade and work in spurts until you have a homogeneous, smooth mixture. Add the wine and process until well mixed.

4. When the cabbage has cooled enough so that you can hold it comfortably, squeeze it to press out water and then dry it with a clean dishtowel.

5. Cut four pieces of string to a length of 30 inches each. Spread them out on a work surface in a starburst pattern so that their midpoints cross and their ends are equally spaced around an imaginary circle. Center one of the sheets of pork fat over the strings. Set the cabbage over the pork fat, core side down. Now, working carefully, to avoid breaking or detaching the leaves, fold them back one by one until the leaves are too small to turn back. Trim out what remains of the stalk.

6. Now apply the stuffing. Keep dipping your hands in cold water as you work to facilitate handling the sticky forcemeat. First put a dab in the center of the cabbage. Stick back the trimmings from the stalk. Put another dab of stuffing on top of them. Now smear two or three of the innermost leaves and pull up to their original position, pull up a few more leaves, smear them, and continue in this manner until you have coated all the leaves except the outermost layer. Pull up these outer leaves and press the cabbage into its pristine shape.

7. Place the second sheet of pork fat over the reconstituted cabbage. Now knot the strings tightly at the top of the cabbage, producing a melonlike package.

8. Spread the sliced onion and carrot over the bottom of a pot just large enough to hold the cabbage. Set the cabbage over them, stalk side down. At this point, you can refrigerate the cabbage until you are ready to finish cooking it. It should keep well for 24 hours.

9. Roughly 4 hours before you want to serve the cabbage, preheat the oven to 350 degrees. Pour the stock over the cabbage. Set over high heat and bring to a boil. When this happens, set a piece of greased wax paper over the cabbage, cover the pot, and put it in the oven. Leave it there, bubbling slowly for 3 ½ hours. After 15 minutes, check the liquid and adjust the oven temperature if necessary to prevent a vigorous boil. Add water as necessary to maintain the liquid level.

10. To serve: Drain the cabbage in a colander. Cut and discard the strings and the pork fat. Keep warm while you reduce the strained cooking liquid to a cup or a touch less.

11. Put the cabbage on a round plate or a large shallow soup bowl. Pour the reduced cooking liquid over it.

Serves 6 to 8

carrots

took it as a sign of evolutionary progress when my sons both ate carrots without hesitation, with enthusiasm in fact, from infancy. Carrots, especially cooked carrots, had repelled me as a child, mushy orange things lurking in stews. I would push them to the side of my plate, and this was tolerated, since carrots were the only common food I actively disliked. Had I lived a few centuries earlier, *Daucus carota* would not have plagued me.

In antiquity, the carrot as we know it—an orange root vegetable with a high sugar content—did not exist.

The earliest reference, from ancient Babylonia, suggests that carrots were first cultivated for their aromatic leaves and seeds. Anyone who has seen a flowering carrot will remember the graceful umbrella-shaped "umbel" sprouting from the top.

This is the sign that carrots are members of the Umbelliferae family, like fennel, coriander, and other plants exploited for their pungent seeds.

Only much later in human history, long after Arabs brought the carrot to Europe through Spain, did the originally unpalatable and often purple carrot of yore get hybridized into the sapid orange variety we take to be the only natural carrot today. That variety (*sativa*) gets its color from beta carotene (which humans metabolize into vitamin A) and, Davidson says, was first described in the Netherlands in the eighteenth century, although it appears in Dutch paintings of the seventeenth.

Carrots can be eaten raw, as sticks or shredded into salads. The classic French recipe for cooking carrots on their own is to boil them in water with sugar until the carrots soften and the liquid reduces to a sweet glaze (carrots Vichy). Carrots are often added to stews and soups for flavoring. They are an essential ingredient in the haute cuisine *appareil* (a sort of chef's condiment) called *mirepoix*, which is a mixture of carrots, onion, ham, and herbs named after the Duke of Mirepoix, a hapless figure who essentially sold his wife to Louis XV. His title derives from a mini-region between Toulouse and the Pyrenees full of pretty battlements, castles, and Romanesque churches. Restaurants in the Mirepoix area serve cassoulet, foie gras, and other specialties of southwest France. Carrots are not mentioned prominently in accounts of the Mirepoix.

In non-Western cultures, carrots are often pickled. You will find them lighting up preserved Mexican jalapeño peppers. Indians convert them into a searingly hot condiment. Quite at the other end of the taste scale is the international menu of carrot sweets. Indians dote on carrot halvah and carrot *kheer*, a milk pudding. Carrot cake is a favorite of the dietarily pious the world over, but the Swiss can properly claim to have got there first with *Aargauer Rüblitorte*. Hochdeutsch for carrot is *Mohrrübe*, meaning Moorish root vegetable, which suggests that it came to Germany from Moorish Andalusia. The standard Spanish word for carrot, *zanahoria*, is a corruption of the Arabic for parsnip. "Carrot" derives from Silver Latin *carota*, which could not have meant carrot in our sense when Apicius used it in his Roman cookbook. So the transmission of *D. carota* from the Near East to Europe through Spain by Arabs is confirmed by all three of these words in different ways. The Spanish word reflects confusion over which root vegetable Arab speakers were talking about. The German term is an obvious tag denoting the Arab source of an exotic vegetable. And the Latin word spread by Roman legions to France and Britain must have been transferred, from whatever precarrot it was originally applied to, onto the superior Andalusian carrot brought in from the south.

potage crécy

The French town most famously associated with the carrot is Crécy,* a village in the department of the Somme in northern France, where Edward III of England defeated Philip of Valois in 1346 during the Hundred Years' War, effectively bringing the era of chivalry to an end. How? Because the English infantry deployed the Welsh longbow to murderous effect against mounted French knights in armor. This tactic was not considered an example of *le fairplay* by the French,† but it revolutionized the art of war. None of this explains the apparently arbitrary association of the carrot with Crécy. But it is a fact that if you order something *à la Crécy* on a traditional French menu, you may be sure that you will soon be tasting carrot.‡ Most often, this will be a potage, a thick soup made from pureed carrots.

½ pound bread crusts, with a quarter inch of bread attached
¾ pound carrots, peeled and trimmed
¼ pound butter
1 medium onion, peeled and finely chopped
6 cups defatted chicken stock
3 parsley sprigs
2½ teaspoons sugar
1 cup raw long-grain unconverted rice
Salt
1 tablespoon chopped chervil (or parsley), for a garnish

1. Dice the crusts and dry out in a toaster oven but don't let them brown.
2. With a vegetable peeler, cut the carrots into thin shavings.
3. Melt half the butter in a heavy saucepan. When the foam subsides, add the carrot shavings and the chopped onion. Stir to coat the carrot pieces and onion with the butter. Then reduce the heat to low, cover, and sweat for around 10 minutes, or until the carrots have totally softened. Stir regularly to prevent sticking and browning.
4. Add the toasted bread pieces, 4 cups of the stock, and the 3 sprigs of parsley. Bring to a boil, reduce the heat, and simmer slowly for 40 minutes.
5. Meanwhile, bring 6 cups of lightly salted water to a boil, add the rice, and simmer until al dente, around 15 minutes. Drain and set aside.
6. Process the carrot mixture and push through a chinois or other very fine strainer into a clean saucepan. Add the rest of the stock and return to the boil. Move the pan to the edge of the burner so as to concentrate the bubbling of the soup to a single point.

Using a soupspoon, remove the scum that rises for 15 to 20 minutes. You can refrigerate the soup at this point if you aren't ready to serve it.

7. When you are ready to serve the soup, reheat if necessary, swirl in the rest of the butter, and strain it a second time through the chinois into a tureen.

8. Add the rice, heat through, stir into the soup, season with salt, and sprinkle with the chervil (or parsley).

Serves 6 to 8

*There are actually several Crécys in France. Ours, the *ville-carotte*, so to speak, is fully denominated Crécy-en-Ponthieu, to distinguish it from the others. It lies a few kilometers from the English Channel just south of Calais in Picardy, through which the fast train Eurostar now whizzes toward the Chunnel, ignoring the site of that momentous bloody Saturday 750 years ago.

†By one account, the French showed their contempt for their horseless foe by mooning them. The English let fly their arrows at these splendid targets, giving the French a major pain *au cul*.

‡French menu language is a code, a system of signs, usually adjectives of place or nationality entirely unrelated to their normal signification. Robert Graves described a similar situation in *Goodbye to All That*, his 1929 memoir of World War I. In the British army, he recalled, the word "fucking" was merely a signal that a noun was coming next.

aargauer rüblitorte
swiss carrot cake

Aargau is a northern Swiss canton on the German border, west of Zurich. The name means the district of the river Aar. Rübli is the Swiss-German diminutive of the Hochdeutsch word for root vegetable, *Rübe*. There are many other carrot cake recipes in the world, but this is the most famous and the most delicious. It is certainly one of Switzerland's very few contributions to world cuisine.*

Butter for the cake pan

6 eggs, separated

1 cup sugar

2 pounds carrots, peeled and grated

Grated peel and juice of ½ lemon

½ pound ground almonds

⅓ cup flour, sifted together with 1 teaspoon baking powder

1 pinch salt

1 tablespoon kirsch

Confectioners' sugar

1. Preheat the oven to 325 degrees and butter the inside of a 9-inch cake pan.

2. Beat the egg yolks with the sugar until smooth and lemon-yellow in color. Then beat in the grated carrots, the lemon peel and juice, the ground almonds, the flour–baking powder mixture, the salt, and the kirsch until well mixed.

3. Beat the egg whites until stiff but not dry. Fold into the yolk mixture and then scrape into the cake pan.

4. Bake for about 1 hour, until the top is lightly browned and the sides have begun pulling away from the cake pan.

5. Let the cake cool on a rack. Hold a serving plate over the cake and invert the cake onto it. Dust with confectioners' sugar and serve

Serves 8

*The only others that come immediately to mind are cheese fondue and that other après-ski cheese dish *raclette*; Zürich *Geschnetzeltes*, a stew of veal strips and mushrooms, and its frequent accompaniment, *rösti* potatoes, Swiss hash browns. Should you be inclined to identify this dish to guests, just say *R-gower Roobleetort*. Or invite a Swiss to say it for you. In a pinch, "Swiss carrot cake" will do.

cassava

f this native root
vegetable of the New World tropics did not have a Linnaean name—*Manihot esculenta*—we would be forced to navigate among four vernacular names, all of them descendants of Amerindian terms for the same starchy plant. In modern U.S. English, *manioc* is the least used and therefore sounds exotic and Amazonian. Indeed, it enters the culinary vocabulary in Brazil as *mandioca*, especially in connection with the flour, *farinha de mandioca*, served toasted (and then referred to as *farofa*) with the Brazilian national bean stew, *feijoada*. *Cassava* is, especially in the English-speaking Caribbean, a flat bread made from manioc flour. *Tapioca* is tapioca, the processed little balls that precipitate out of liquefied manioc flour when it is heated. Finally, *yuca* is the word for *M. esculenta* in Spanish. Since

hispanophones are the principal buyers of this 15-inch-long tuber, yuca is what it is called in U.S. markets. Non-Spanish North Americans fall easily into the mistake of confusing yuca with yucca, an unrelated member of the agave family. Yuca is pronounced *you kah*. But yucca sounds like *yuk kah*.*

Starchy, low in protein, cassava is hard to cook without producing third-world library paste. Treated well, it offers an elastic texture its admirers (I am one) find voluptuous.

*Yucca Flat, Nev., was part of the testing ground for nuclear weapons northwest of Las Vegas.

carimañolas
colombian-panamanian cassava fritters*

In Cartagena de Indias, where the fortifications that once held the treasures of the Spanish Empire still face the Caribbean shore of Colombia, a polyglot cuisine developed, a mix of indigenous, African, and Spanish ideas and ingredients. *Carimañolas* are a trademark dish of the region, which extends westward into Panama. Like empanadas or pakoras, they are stuffed savory pastries. The difference is that the dough is created from mashed cassava, rolled around a chilified, chopped-meat picadillo, and then shaped into a sort of torpedo. In her recipe the preeminent Cartagenan cook Teresita Roman de Zurek says that a carimañola should look like a blimp, *como un dirigible*.

½ pound ground pork

½ pound ground beef

1 onion, peeled and chopped

2 garlic cloves, peeled and chopped

3 dried red chiles, seeded

1 tablespoon vinegar

¼ teaspoon ground cumin

Salt

Pepper

3 cups oil or lard for frying

2½ pounds cassava (yuca), peeled and cut into chunks

1. Put the pork, beef, onion, garlic, chiles, vinegar, cumin, salt, and pepper in the bowl of a processor with ½ cup of water and mix well.

2. Heat ¼ cup of the oil or lard with a tablespoon of salt in a saucepan large enough to hold the yuca in a single layer. Add the yuca chunks and cover. Let the yuca chunks simmer until they have softened just enough to run a fork through them.

3. While the yuca is still hot, process in short spurts until it turns into a smooth dough.

*Adapted from Teresita Roman de Zurek's *Cartagena de Indias en la Olla* (Bogota: Gamma, 18th edition, 1988).

4. Moisten your hands and roll into 12 balls. Flatten the balls and stuff each one with about ¼ cup of the ground-meat mixture. Close the balls around the stuffing and form into torpedo-shaped bundles.

5. Heat the remaining oil or lard until it just begins to smoke. Fry the carimañolas three at a time until nicely browned. Drain in a wire basket or on paper toweling. Serve as soon as possible.

Serves 6

enyucado
colombian cassava confection

I first encountered this little cake in a bar in Cartagena on the Colombian national day. I noticed a plate of little nondescript squares sitting on the bar. The man I asked about them muttered something that seemed to have no consonants. Eventually, I got him to write down *enyucado*, which literally means en-yuca-ed. And there's no denying that. Or that enyucados are not only delicious bar snacks but also a fine dessert. The coconut is typical of this former slave-worked coast. The underlying cake ingredients as well as the aniseed hispanify the basic raw material, grated cassava, which is as American as apple pie. Actually more so.

Butter for the brownie pan

1½ pounds cassava, peeled and finely grated

1 cup sugar

6 ounces white cheese (*queso blanco* or *queso del país*), grated

1 tablespoon butter, melted

1 cup coconut milk (see Note)

2 teaspoons aniseeds

2 tablespoons heavy cream

1. Preheat the oven to 350 degrees and butter the inside of a 6-cup brownie pan.
2. Whisk together the grated yuca, sugar, grated cheese, and butter. Then work in the coconut milk.
3. Rub the aniseeds together in your hands to release their aroma. Then stir them into the yuca mixture. Finally, stir in the heavy cream and continue stirring until you have a smooth dough.
4. Turn the dough into the brownie pan and bake in the oven for 40 minutes, or until nicely browned. Cut into squares and serve.

Serves 6

Note: There are three ways to acquire coconut milk:

1. You can buy it in cans, a form popular in all countries that traditionally use coconut milk.
2. You can buy a coconut, crack the shell, save the liquid, and separate the white meat from the shell. Grate the meat over a bowl. Then press the grated meat in a strainer, a handful at a time, to extract the milk. Reserve the pressed coconut meat in

a bowl. Add the milk to the coconut liquid. If you don't have a cup, moisten the grated meat with a little water and press again. Repeat, if necessary, until you have a cup of coconut milk.

3. Process the grated coconut meat with the liquid. Then press the milk through a strainer and, if necessary, add some water and proceed as above in step 2.

crème de tapioca com pêssego
tapioca cream with peaches

In Brazil, where tapioca comes from, they dress it up with peaches, walnuts, and cream, an Amazonian sundae.

¼ cup tapioca
½ teaspoon salt
½ cup sugar
1 egg yolk, lightly beaten
Juice of ½ lemon
6 ripe peaches, peeled, halved, and pitted
½ cup chopped walnuts
½ cup heavy cream

1. Soak the tapioca in 4 cups cold water for 2 hours.
2. Drain. Add the salt to the boiling water and then stir in the tapioca. Lower the heat and simmer until the tapioca has swelled fully, about 20 minutes, stirring constantly.
3. Stir in the sugar. When it has dissolved, beat ½ cup of the tapioca liquid into the egg. Mix well and then beat into the tapioca mixture. Continue cooking over low-medium heat until the mixture thickens.
4. Remove from the heat immediately and stir in the lemon juice. Then stir in the peaches and the chopped walnuts. Mix well and let cool to room temperature.
5. Whip the cream to the Chantilly stage, until it forms soft peaks but does not completely stiffen.
6. Put the tapioca cream into six individual goblets or dishes. Cover with whipped cream and refrigerate.

Serves 6

cauliflower

Mark Twain observed that the cauliflower is a cabbage with a college education. This was not just a quip. Cauliflower is a member of the cabbage family, Cruciferae, so-named because of their cross-shaped flowers. Indeed, it is a member of the same genus, *Brassica*, and the same species, *oleracea*, as cabbage. To distinguish these cultivars, cabbage is further classified in the Capitata group and cauliflower in the Botrytis group.* Twain, despite his lack of college education, must have known about this taxonomic connection, as did the people in France and Spain, whose words for cauliflower, *chou-fleur* and *coliflor*, translate literally as cabbage flower. Cauliflower itself obviously

chou-fleur à la polonaise 72

*It is not, however, related to the beneficial fungus *Botrytis cinerea*, which grows on late-harvest grapes and improves their flavor. In the vineyards of Sauternes, where it is rife, this Botrytis is known as the noble rot, *la pourriture noble*.

contains the same Romance root for cabbage, which also surfaces in Coleslaw (page 53).

If you look closely at a cauliflower, you will see outer green leaves that are essentially cabbage leaves. In the field, they are wrapped around the plant's flower so that it will not receive light from the sun and turn the developing "curd" green. This milky curd is the flower of cauliflower. Actually, there are green varieties in the market (broccoflower) and even an orange one with enhanced vitamin A. But the white cauliflower is the classic and overwhelmingly prevalent type.

It is nutritionally excellent and also low in calories and cholesterol. The curd, moreover, is a fractal, which is to say that its flowerets are indistinguishable from the whole curd except in scale.

chou-fleur à la polonaise

Why is this dish called Polish in French cookbooks? Polish sources do not mention it. As so often with traditional French terminology, *à la polonaise* simply reflects some French notion of Polish food. Why should a combination of browned bread crumbs, chopped eggs, and butter have struck anyone as especially Polish? In the words of Montaigne, *Que sais-je?**

8 tablespoons butter, melted
¾ cup bread crumbs
1 large cauliflower, trimmed
3 hard-boiled eggs, shelled and finely chopped
1 tablespoon finely chopped parsley

1. Heat half the butter in a skillet and brown the bread crumbs in it. Set aside.
2. Steam the cauliflower in 2 inches of boiling water, covered, until a knife can just slide through the cauliflower, about 20 to 25 minutes.
3. Drain the cauliflower and set in a serving dish. Sprinkle the chopped eggs and the bread crumbs over it. Then pour on the remaining melted butter and sprinkle with parsley.

Serves 6

*What do I know? A seemingly obvious line, but it is the great thinker-essayist's most quoted state-ment, so famous that it is customarily included in language textbooks to illustrate the inversion of subject and object in French questions, and it became the title of an entire line of informational paper-backs in France.

celeriac

Often called just plain "celery root," celeriac, *Apium graveolens* var. *rapaceum*, is indeed the enlarged, spheroid root of the celery grown for its stalks, *A. graveolens* var. *dulce*. The first written references to it date from the sixteenth century in Europe and suggest that this variety was first cultivated in the Old World, perhaps in the Arab world. Celeriac, once peeled and sliced into matchsticks or very thin disks, can be eaten raw in salads. This sounds simpler than it is, since the gnarly, softball-sized root takes more care and heft with the peeler than a potato.

Céleri rémoulade, by far the most famous recipe, takes raw celeriac matchsticks and softens them overnight in a mustard vinaigrette called *rémoulade*, which means reground. Why this should be is a mystery unexplained by standard sources. It may descend from an earlier version of the sauce in which herbs were ground particularly fine. The similar sauce often served with shrimp in New Orleans is pink from paprika.

Cooked celery root can be served as a puree. In the classic version, mashed potatoes are added for smoothness. The earthy flavor of celery root survives this adulteration.

céleri rémoulade

1½ pounds celeriac
½ cup Dijon mustard
¼ cup white wine vinegar
1 cup canola oil
1 garlic clove, peeled and pushed through a garlic press
Salt and pepper

1. Peel the celeriac. Then cut it into the thinnest possible julienne strips.
2. Put the mustard in a mixing bowl. Whisk in the vinegar. Then whisk in the canola oil, starting with a very small amount and progressing to larger increments as the sauce emulsifies or thickens. This is the same technique used to make mayonnaise.
3. When all the oil is incorporated, whisk in the pureed garlic and salt and pepper to taste.
4. With a wooden spoon or spatula, stir a small amount of the julienned celeriac into the mustard sauce. Then stir in the rest. Let stand, covered, in the refrigerator for 24 hours, to soften the celeriac. Let the dish return to room temperature before serving.

Serves 6

mashed celeriac and potatoes

Salt

½ pound celeriac

2 pounds potatoes

4 garlic cloves, peeled and finely chopped

6 tablespoons room-temperature butter, sliced

White pepper

1. Boil 3 quarts of water and ¼ cup salt in a Dutch oven or couscousière.

2. Peel and dice the celeriac. Add to the boiling water and simmer for 20 minutes.

3. Peel and quarter the potatoes. Add them to the water along with the garlic, and simmer for another 10 minutes, or until the potato pieces are soft.

4. Drain in a colander. Transfer to a large mixing bowl and mash thoroughly. Do not use a food processor because it will turn the puree into library paste. A hand masher or a potato ricer will speed the job.

5. Put the puree in a saucepan. Set over medium heat and stir while excess moisture steams away. When the puree begins to coat the spoon and the sides of the pan, remove from the heat and stir in the butter to smooth it. Season to taste with salt and white pepper.

Serves 6 to 8

chard

Chard (*Beta vulgaris,* Cicla group) is a cultivated form of beet grown for its celerylike stalk and its spinachlike leaves. There is a red-stalked variety called ruby chard. The name "chard" itself is related to the Latin for thistle, although it is botanically not a thistle. Because of this and other nomenclatural confusions, especially in French where *charde* is a general term for the leaf rib of chard or the cardoon, chard itself is known variously as *bette*, *blète*, or *blette* (this last term is particularly confusing because it is a homonym in French for the feminine of the adjective *blet (blette)*, which refers to an overripe fruit and is a cognate of the English word *bletting*, the process by which medlars are gathered and left to overripen to the consistency of applesauce, which improves their taste).

No wonder then that people interested in selling chard have long been calling it Swiss chard, if for no other reason than to set it off as a veg unto itself, there being no known connection with Switzerland. The subspecies name has been explained as deriving from *sicula* (Latin for Sicilian) on the supposition that it entered Europe from Sicily as a result of commerce with North Africa. Davidson supports this etymology while also putting forth an even more persuasive connection with the plant's Arabic name, *silq*, the source of the Spanish chard word *acelga*. This second etymology looks to me like the explanation for both linguistic pathways. Chard definitely came to Europe from the Near East with the Moors, and a simple transposition of consonants yields sicula/cicla from silq.

A chard by any name, however derived, presents the cook with the same "issue," namely whether to eat the stalks or the leaves, see the next recipe.

labaneya
chard and yogurt soup

This Egyptian soup recipe eschews stalks and leaf veins. Even the simplest treatment of chard entails cooking the stalks and ribs separately from the leaves. For example, the leaves can be steamed like spinach, while the stalks and veins can be chopped and sautéed like celery. This offers the choice of serving the leaves at one meal and the stalks and veins at another or, in a modern twist, serving them together as a kind of vegetable pun. Either way, chard offers you a twofer (unless, of course, you want to make a separate dish out of the veins, a naturally julienned oddment that one guest in ten thousand will identify for what it is).

2 pounds chard (to yield 1 pound leaves)

1 onion, peeled and finely chopped

1 leek, white part only, washed and sliced in thin rounds

2 tablespoons olive oil

¾ cup long-grain rice, washed and drained

Salt and pepper

½ teaspoon turmeric

2 cups yogurt

3 garlic cloves, peeled and pushed through a garlic press

1. Trim away the white stems from the chard leaves. Then cut the central vein out of the leaves. Set the leaves aside. Either discard the stems and veins or, much better, thriftier and wiser, sauté them in butter as a vegetable side dish.

2. Sauté the onion and the leek in olive oil until lightly colored. Add the trimmed chard leaves and cook until wilted, stirring.

3. Transfer the chard mixture to a large pot. Add 5 cups of water, the rice, salt and pepper to taste, and the turmeric. Bring to a boil and simmer until the rice is al dente, at least 10 minutes.

4. Meanwhile, stir the yogurt and garlic together in a bowl. When the rice is done, stir the yogurt into the soup. When you are ready to serve the soup, heat but do not boil it. Yogurt curdles when boiled.

Serves 6

mehshi sille ^
lebanese stuffed swiss chard leaves

Use the stuffing below not only for chard leaves, but also vine leaves, seeded zucchini, or bell peppers. The method of cooking is almost the same in all cases: The stuffed leaves or vegetables are immersed in water and simmered for 45 minutes, or until the stuffing is cooked. The most famous of these dishes is stuffed vine leaves, but I am offering a recipe for stuffed Swiss chard leaves instead, because fresh vine leaves are not available to most people, and preserved vine leaves, even when well soaked, are to the fresh leaves as canned peas are to fresh peas.

2 ¾ pounds Swiss chard
2 large ripe tomatoes, peeled and thinly sliced
1 recipe Lebanese Vegetable Stuffing (page 82)
Salt

1. Cut the stems off the chard leaves and reserve. Then cut the leaves into three parts. First, make a cut perpendicular to the vein at the point where the vein thickens. You can find this point by rolling down the leaf from the top. The place on the vein where the leaf no longer rolls easily is the place to make your cut. Now cut away the vein from the lower part of the leaf. This will yield the second and third sections of trimmed leaf. Reserve the veins with the stems. Continue in this manner until you have cut all the leaves into three parts. Very small leaves can simply be deveined, i.e., divided in half.

2. Blanch the reserved stems and veins in boiling water. Drain.

3. Cover the bottom of a large casserole with the tomato slices. Sprinkle the blanched stems and veins on top of the tomato layer.

4. Now stuff and roll the leaves: Lay a leaf section, smooth side down, with the cut side nearest to you. Take a tablespoon of stuffing (or more for larger leaves) and make a thin line running parallel to the edge of the leaf nearest you, about ½ inch inside the leaf. The line of stuffing should begin and end about ½ inch from the sides of the leaf. Fold the narrow lower strip of leaf over the stuffing and then roll up the leaf into a loosely packed tube (this allows for expansion of the rice as it cooks). Press the unfilled ends flat and place the stuffed leaf, cut side down, over the stems in the casserole.

5. Continue in this manner until you have used up either the stuffing or the leaves. Cook leftover stuffing in simmering water and serve on the side. Use leftover leaves to

cover the stuffed leaves in the casserole. Pour enough water over the leaves so that it just covers them. Add salt to taste.

6. Lay a plate over the leaves to keep them stationary while they cook. Bring the water to a boil over high heat, reduce to a simmer, cover, and cook for 45 minutes, or until the rice is soft. After 20 minutes, taste the broth and add salt if necessary.

7. Let the stuffed leaves cool in the broth. Carefully transfer the leaves to a serving dish. Serve at room temperature. Pass some of the broth as a sauce.

Serves 6 to 8

hashweh bil-zeit
lebanese vegetable stuffing

⅔ cup short-grain (risotto) rice

1½ pounds tomatoes, roughly chopped

6 scallions, trimmed and thinly sliced

Leaves from 1 small bunch flat-leaf parsley, roughly chopped

⅓ cup mint leaves, roughly chopped

3 tablespoons sumac

½ teaspoon ground cinnamon

½ teaspoon ground allspice

Salt and pepper

Juice of 1 large lemon

⅓ cup olive oil

Wash the rice in three changes of cold water. Drain and put in a mixing bowl. Then add all the remaining ingredients. Mix well. Adjust the seasoning.

chayote

n New Orleans, for
reasons lost in the Delta mists since
Napoleon sold the place to Jefferson in 1803,
they call this pale-green, delicate vegetable
mirliton, standard French for a toy reed
flute. Elsewhere in areas of former French
domination, this cousin of gourds, melons,
and squashes is a *christophine*. In Spanish-
speaking areas, it takes its Mexican name,
chayote, from the Nahuatl *chayotl*. My
mother knew it as the vegetable pear. It
appears sporadically in U.S. supermarkets,
identifiable mainly because it doesn't look
like anything else you've seen, with its
nobbled, ridged pale green skin. The flesh is
paler still and, when cooked, has an
evanescent mild squashy taste. In the center
is a flat, white nutlike seed said to be edible.

Mother learned to cook vegetable pears
from her Jamaican friend Cora Pratt. They

met at an NAACP meeting that Mother attended not so much out of enthusiasm for the "Negro" cause, but because she was desperate for human company (my father had not yet returned from his stint as a Public Health Service syphilologist at Fort Bliss outside El Paso) and was seven months pregnant with my sister, bored and lonely. She had read about the meeting in the NAACP magazine *Crisis* (my parents got it as a benefit for their annual check to the NAACP) and decided to take a cab downtown to the Hannan YMCA, where it would be held.

This was, for someone who had been fearful about encountering anti-Semitism in officers' clubs and had never in her life designed to be on an equal social footing with a black person, a rather bold plan.

The Checker cabdriver didn't want to take her, but in the end he relented; she sat in the back of the meeting on a bench, feeling uncomfortable and awkward. Cora was sitting next to her in her khaki WAC's uniform, including the hat. They fell to chatting about military life when the meeting broke up. Cora drove Mom home. The friendship lasted until Mom discovered Cora in her bed without the uniform. Daddy was taking a shower. From then on in our house, vegetable pear on the table was a tacit reproach. I found out about this from Inez the laundress, who came up from Black Bottom in Detroit's ghetto to run sheets through the mangle in the basement.

Inez . . . well, that's another story.

gratin de christophine
martinican baked stuffed chayote

The global French *mission civilisatrice* has left its refined mark on *Sechiumedule* in this recipe, which is Old World in every way except for its main ingredient. But gentle as the chayote is in essence, its yielding tropical nature pervades the dish.

Salt

3 large chayotes

4 slices stale white bread, without crusts

3 tablespoons milk

½ pound bacon, diced

1 onion, peeled and chopped

3 scallions, trimmed and chopped

4 flat-leaf parsley sprigs, finely chopped

1 thyme sprig

¼ cup oil, approximately

Salt

Pepper

3 tablespoons butter

⅓ cup grated Gruyère cheese

1 tablespoon dried bread crumbs

1. Bring 8 cups of lightly salted water to a boil. Cut the chayotes in half and simmer for 20 to 30 minutes in the water until quite tender.

2. Drain the chayotes. Remove and discard the peel and the almond-shaped seeds.

3. Puree the chayote flesh in a processor. Reserve.

4. Chop the stale bread into crumbs. In a bowl, soak the crumbs in the milk. Reserve.

5. Preheat the oven to 425 degrees.

6. Heat the bacon in a skillet. When it has rendered its fat but before it browns, add the onion and scallions. Now brown the bacon along with the onion and scallions.

7. Stir the chayote puree into the bacon mixture, as well as the parsley. Strip the leaves off the thyme and stir them in with salt and pepper to taste. Cook over low

heat, stirring until the texture of the puree is smooth. Add up to ¼ cup oil if necessary.

8. Meanwhile, butter a 6-cup gratin pan. When the puree is ready, spread it in the pan. Sprinkle with the Gruyère and bread crumbs. Cut the rest of the butter into small pieces and scatter on top.

9. Set the pan in the middle of the oven for around 10 minutes, until the "gratin" is nicely browned. Serve immediately.

Serves 4

cuban chayote pudding

Spain here colonizes the chayote with typically peninsular ingredients such as ground almonds and by making a flan with its processed flesh.

4 large chayotes, sliced in half lengthwise
Salt
4 tablespoons cornstarch
1⅓ cups milk
1 cinnamon stick
Peel of 1 lemon
4 egg yolks
1⅓ cups sugar
1½ teaspoons vanilla
⅔ cup raisins
⅔ cup ground almonds

1. Bring 8 cups of lightly salted water to a boil. Add the chayote halves, return to the boil, reduce the heat, and simmer until tender, 20 to 30 minutes.

2. Drain the chayotes. As soon as they are cool enough to handle, spoon out the flesh and reserve, being careful not to damage the peels. Discard the seeds.

3. Dissolve the cornstarch in the milk. Pour into the processor and add the chayote flesh and process until smooth. Transfer to a saucepan. Add the stick of cinnamon, the lemon peel, the egg yolks, and the sugar. Stir together and heat over medium heat until the custard thickens. Remove from the heat and immerse the pan in cold water to stop the cooking. Stir to cool for a couple of minutes. Remove the cinnamon stick and the lemon peel and discard.

4. Stir in the vanilla and the raisins. Spoon this mixture into the chayote peels (put any excess in a serving bowl). Chill for several hours before serving. Meanwhile, toast the ground almonds in a 300-degree oven until lightly browned. When ready to serve, sprinkle the custard with the almonds.

Serves 8

chickpeas

Cicer arietinum is an ancient cultivar thoroughly documented as far back as 6000 B.C. in Middle Eastern archeological sites and much cherished in ancient Greece and Rome. Virgil mentioned it in his salad poem *Moretum* (see page 196). Marcus Tullius Cicero, the greatest Latin prose stylist and a leading politician of the late Republic (106–43 B.C.), is nicknamed after the chickpea.* The Latin name survives in Italian *ceci* and in chickpea. The Spanish name *garbanzo* derives from the Greek *erebinthos* (ἐρέβυνθος), mentioned in *The Iliad* 13.589.† Hummus is the Arabic.

*Roman names came in three parts. In order, they were the *praenomen*, equivalent to our first name; the *nomen*, or family name; and the *cognomen*, the equivalent of a nickname: Publius Clodius Pulcher (beautiful), a decadent public figure; Publius Ovidius Naso (nose), the poet Ovid; Cnaeus Pompeius Strabo (squinty), the geographer.

†"Just as dark-fleshed beans and chickpeas leap off the threshing floor sped by shrill wind and a strong winnower, so bitter arrows ricochet off the breastplate of noble Menelaus and fly far off."

hummus bi tahini
lebanese chickpea puree with sesame cream

Anissa Helou, like any Lebanese, has a special attachment to chickpeas. They are an indigenous vegetable all over the Mediterranean. We know this because early Greek poetry refers to them, and they are the essential ingredient in the most fundamental food of the Levant, the tahini-flavored puree known throughout the world as hummus.

Chickpeas start out looking a bit like garden-variety peas. As Helou writes in *Lebanese Cuisine* (1998): "There is a short moment in early summer when chick peas are available fresh. Green bunches laden with the peas still in the pod are sold by street hawkers, usually to children who spend hours squeezing each pod open to extract and eat the green chick peas. A very healthy snack."

Chickpea flour is a traditional staple in Nice and elsewhere, all the way to India, where it is called *gram*. But the world recipe is hummus. It is everywhere now, in degraded industrial, flavored hummus products that give no inkling of the "smooth ivory" texture Helou talks about. And, almost as important as the basic preparation of the puree, is the ingenious traditional method of serving (see steps 5 and 6 below) in which hummus spread out on a shallow plate is mounded slightly at the edges and the center, creating a natural receptacle for olive oil and a platform for displaying a few whole chickpeas.

This arrangement was clearly designed for a circle of people all scooping up hummus and moistening it in oil with a little pouch of pita bread held in the right hand. It also looks beautiful, and it inspires thoughts of Arab hospitality going back centuries.

Tahini is the other crucial ingredient, a thick "cream" made from pressed, roasted sesame seeds. Quality varies greatly among brands; Helou favors imported tahini from the eastern Mediterranean. You can easily test this proposition by staging a blind tahini tasting. Then serve rosewater-tinged martinis and make hummus to go with them from the tahini brand you have picked.

2 cups dried chickpeas

3 garlic cloves, peeled and minced

Juice of 2 large or 3 small lemons, about ½ cup

1 cup tahini

Salt

½ teaspoon cayenne (optional)

1½ teaspoons ground cumin or paprika, to sprinkle on the hummus

2 to 3 tablespoons olive oil

Pita wedges

1. Soak the chickpeas overnight.

2. Boil the chickpeas in plenty of water for at least an hour until they can be mashed with a fork.

3. Save ½ cup of the cooking water. Drain away the rest and put the chickpeas and the ½ cup water in the jar of a blender (reserving 6 chickpeas for a garnish) with the garlic and half the lemon juice. Blend until smooth. Scrape into a mixing bowl.

4. Work in the tahini and beat until completely mixed. The color will lighten. Add salt to taste. Add more lemon juice if you want a sourer spread. Add the cayenne if you want a bit of heat.

5. When you are ready to serve the hummus, spread it over a shallow plate. Run the back of a serving spoon in a circle through the hummus so as to leave a trough between the center and the edge. Put the reserved chickpeas on the mound at the center.

6. Heat the cumin briefly in the olive oil. Then drizzle it around the trough in the hummus. Sprinkle additional cumin or paprika around the raised outer rim of the hummus.

Serves 6 to 8 as an hors d'oeuvre with pita

masaledar chhole
spicy indian chickpeas

India has many snack foods. This one is a showcase for spices, which work a symphonic magic on the ground bass of the unassertive chickpea. I suggest using dried chickpeas although canned chickpeas are entirely acceptable, if a bit soft.

1½ pounds dried chickpeas

1 pinch baking soda

One 2-inch piece fresh ginger, peeled

5 tablespoons lemon juice

1 medium onion

2 medium tomatoes

9 black cardamoms

One 2½-inch cinnamon stick

5 cloves

1 ounce, or about 3 inches ginger, smashed

7 black tea leaves

5 tablespoons non-olive oil

½ teaspoon *ajwain* (carom) seeds

3 tablespoons chickpea flour (gram or *besan* flour)

2 tablespoons pomegranate seeds

2½ teaspoons dried mango powder

1½ teaspoons cayenne

1½ teaspoons black salt

2 tablespoons dried fenugreek leaves (*kasoori methi*)

2 teaspoons ground cumin

Salt

6 small green chiles

1. Soak the chickpeas overnight in 2 quarts of cold water.

2. Drain the chickpeas over a large saucepan. Bring their soaking water to a boil with the baking soda. Simmer the chickpeas in the water for 20 minutes until just barely tender.

3. Meanwhile, slice the ginger piece into julienne strips. Set to soak in the lemon juice. Reserve. Peel the onion and slice it. Quarter the tomatoes. Reserve the onion slices and the tomato quarters.

4. Drain the chickpeas and return to the saucepan.

5. Tie up the black cardamoms, cinnamon, cloves, crushed ginger, and tea leaves in a small piece of cheesecloth.

6. Heat 3 tablespoons of the oil in a small skillet and pour over the chickpeas. Toss in the pouch of spices. Stir a few times, cover, and sweat until the chickpeas are tender but not mushy, about 10 minutes. Remove from the heat, discard the spice pouch, and set the chickpeas aside.

7. In a large saucepan, heat the remaining 2 tablespoons oil. Toss in the ajwain seeds. Stir over medium heat until the seeds crackle. Stir in the chickpea flour and stir until it gives off a noticeable aroma. Immediately stir in the pomegranate seeds, the mango powder, the cayenne, the black salt, the fenugreek leaves, the cumin, and salt to taste. Stir-fry for 2 minutes. Then add the chickpeas and stir-fry for a few minutes until they are covered with all the ingredients and heated through.

8. Transfer to a serving bowl. Garnish with the ginger strips (drained), the onion slices, the tomato quarters, and the green chiles.

Serves 4 to 6

chiles

Chiles (*Capsicum* spp.) come in many shapes and sizes, sweet, mild, smoked, hot, hotter, hottest. For the most part, they add heat and flavor to a dish but are not its poster ingredient. This is not to downgrade the importance of chiles in cuisines of the Americas or in the myriad countries and cultures from Thailand to Hungary, where they went native after 1492, transforming and invigorating traditional dishes. People around the world learned quickly to love the heat and the varied tastes of chiles. Anyone who has tasted the Martinican fish stew called *blaff* will have carried away an indelible memory of the flavor of the Scotch bonnet or habanero pepper, as well as a respect for its unchallenged status as the hottest chile of them all. Then there is Hungarian paprika in its many grades of heat and special dark flavor. But Mexico is *Capsicum* heartland.

chiles poblanos en nogada
puebla chiles stuffed with pork in walnut sauce

The *chile poblano* is a glistening dark green chile just big enough to stuff. Poblano means that it is associated with the colonial city of Puebla, now a short drive from Mexico City and redolent of its own colonial traditions, rich in colonial architecture, and home of the emblematic Mexican girl, the *China Poblana*, or Pueblan Chinese maiden. In a thousand labels and posters, she wears her colorful outfit and stands for the proud early days of the Manila galleons that plied the Pacific from the Philippines to Acapulco, linking Europe and Asia. From Acapulco, goods were carted across Mexico to ships waiting in the Gulf of Mexico and the Caribbean to sail on to Seville.

With an even stronger flavor of nationalism, the *chile poblano en nogada* represents the Mexican revolt from the Spanish yoke. At least by the standard account, the already routine fusion dish, *chile relleno**, was dressed up with fresh walnuts and a fancy sauce made to show the colors of the new flag: green (chile), red (pomegranate), and white (cream). It may also simply be the case that pomegranates were in season in September, the *mes patria*, so-called because on the sixteenth of that month in 1810, Father Hidalgo rang the tocsin of liberty from his church in Dolores Guanajuato and set the revolution in motion. Either explanation works for me. But if you are grabbed by the historical myth, remember to stand and give the *grito* (the cry) of independence when you serve *chiles poblanos en nogada*: ¡Viva Mexico!

All over the world, Mexicans will be shouting the same words, and if they are in luck, they will have found chiles poblanos to stuff and savor.

12 poblano chiles

1½ pounds boneless pork shoulder, cubed

2 garlic cloves, peeled and chopped

1 medium onion, peeled and chopped

2 tablespoons corn oil

½ cup vinegar

Salt

2 tablespoons lard

1 pound tomatoes, blanched, peeled, seeded, and chopped

3 tablespoons raisins

10 blanched almonds, slivered

10 pitted green olives, chopped

Sugar

Pepper

1 crumbled bay leaf

50 walnuts, shelled (freshly harvested if possible, otherwise soaked in water overnight), with inner skin removed

½ cup Mexican sour cream or crème fraîche

¼ cup sherry

2 pomegranates

1. Toast the chiles over a direct flame or under the broiler until the skins are blackened. Then leave them in a paper bag for 20 minutes. They should now peel easily. After peeling, cut a lengthwise slit in each chile, but leave the stem and the tip end intact. Trim out the internal veins and remove the seeds. Set aside.

2. Cook the pork in lightly salted water to cover, along with half the garlic and onion, for 45 minutes. Drain, reserving the cooking liquid, and chop the pork fine.

3. Heat the corn oil in a large saucepan and add the remaining garlic plus all but a tablespoon of the remaining onion. Add the chiles and toss until the onion is translucent. Then add the vinegar, 1 cup water, and salt to taste. Bring to a boil, reduce the heat, and simmer until the chiles are cooked through, about 10 minutes or less.

4. Meanwhile, finish cooking the stuffing (*el relleno*). Melt the lard in a skillet and add the remaining tablespoon of onion. Sauté until translucent. Then add the pork, the tomatoes, the raisins, the almonds, and the olives. Stir together and add ½ cup of the reserved pork cooking liquid, a small amount of sugar, salt, pepper, and the bay leaf. Bring to a boil, reduce the heat, and simmer until the liquid has almost completely evaporated.

5. Make the walnut sauce (*la nogada*). Chop the nuts very fine and stir together with the sour cream. Then stir in the sherry. The sauce should be thick but pourable. Add more sherry if necessary to create this consistency.

Stuff the chiles with the pork mixture. Arrange them on a serving platter, cover with the sauce, and then sprinkle with pomegranate seeds.

Serves 6

*The indigenous chile is stuffed with post-Hispanic pork.

puree of roasted red peppers

These are mild bell peppers, about the size and shape of a fist. In Italy, they are preserved whole or in large pieces, seeded and stemmed. Then, famously, they are served cold with anchovies. The recipe below takes the process a step further, turning cooked peppers into a luscious puree that can be used per se as a glamorous and colorful sauce with grilled meat or diluted with chicken stock to make a remarkable soup.

6 large red bell peppers
½ cup olive oil, approximately
Salt

1. Preheat the oven to 475 degrees. Line a roasting pan with enough aluminium foil to wrap the peppers in. Put the peppers in the pan and set the pan in the oven. Leave the peppers unwrapped while they cook. It will take at least 30 minutes for the peppers to cook completely. They are done when they lose their shape completely. During this time, turn them with a tongs every 15 minutes.

2. Remove from the oven, wrap with the foil, and let cool. As soon as you can handle them, remove and discard the stems. The skins will peel away easily and should also be discarded along with the seed-bearing cores.

3. Put the peppers in a food processor. Strain the pepper liquid remaining in the roasting pan (there will be quite a lot of this luscious, thick syrup) to catch any remaining seeds and then add the strained liquid to the peppers. Pour in the olive oil and ½ teaspoon salt. Puree.

Makes about 3 cups

corn

f you have eaten corn in all its forms since early childhood, it takes a certain effort of mental detachment to see this modified grass for the weird plant that it is. The tallness, the silk, the tassel, and most of all the ear mark corn off visually and botanically from the other grasses cultivated for their seeds. *Zea mays* most probably began as the wild Mexican grass *teosinte*, but prehistoric human cultivation grossly inflated its seed head into the ear we know, the ear with its dozens of toothsome and nutritious kernels.

Cornmeal, ground from these kernels, can be exploited as tortillas, polenta, tamales, and a bookful of other recipes crucial to human survival. But the kernel is corn's natural, "vegetable" form (in the sense of this book). And here are four recipes that show the corn kernel at its best, sweet yet earthy, soft but holding its shape and color.

corn fritters

Fritter, the word, derives from French *friture* (something deep-fried) by an obvious process of phonological devolution. But on the western shores of the Atlantic, almost anything deep-fried, especially in a batter, is most likely a descendant of African cookery. From Brazil (Acarajes, see page 38) to Martinique (*acras*) to Charleston (hush puppies), fritters are a link to West African foodways that have been adapted to New World conditions. And the major adaptation that occurred in North America was the incorporation of corn into the basic fritter cuisine. This recipe carries the process as far away from the traditional formula as it can go, expanding the basic fritter concept into a beignet formed from eggs, milk, and wheat flour aerated with a modern chemical raising agent. But the unreconstructed kernels lurk inside, *éminences jaunes* that dominate the dish.

3 eggs

¾ cup milk

2¼ cups flour

1 tablespoon baking powder

1½ teaspoons salt

Cayenne

1½ cups corn kernels, cut fresh from the cob

Oil for deep-frying

1. Separate the eggs.

2. In a mixing bowl, stir together the egg yolks, the milk, the flour, the baking powder, the salt, the cayenne to taste, and the corn kernels.

3. Beat the egg whites until they form stiff peaks. Fold them into the yolk-corn mixture.

4. Heat 4 inches of oil in a kadhai, wok, or deep skillet. When the oil starts to smoke, drop a serving spoonful of batter into the oil. Be careful not to splash. You can cook 2 or 3 fritters at a time until they are golden brown. Drain on a paper toweling. Continue frying until all the batter is used up. If you want to do this twice as fast, keep two frying vessels going at the same time.

Serves 8

corn sautéed with onions

By mid-August, when you tire of corn on the cob, sautéing corn kernels is the best way to go on eating corn without coming down with a case of Kornschmerz. Cooking the kernels changes them in a subtle way. And if you have found a cup or two of chanterelles in the woods, throw them into the skillet, too.

6 ears corn, shucked
3 tablespoons butter
2 garlic cloves, peeled and finely chopped
2 medium onions, peeled and chopped
Salt
Pepper

1. Strip the kernels off the ears of corn. The simplest way to do this is to stand the ears on end and slice off the kernels, working from top to bottom. Collect the kernels in a bowl and reserve.

2. Melt the butter in a large skillet over medium heat. When the foam subsides, toss in the garlic and cook until the pieces just begin to color. Add the onions right away, stir briskly to coat all the pieces with butter, then continue cooking until they are translucent.

3. Stir in the corn kernels. Cook for a few minutes until softened. Add salt and pepper to taste and serve.

Serves 3 to 4

corn soup

I used to make this soup by running a knife down each row of kernels and then pressing out the starchy "milk." This is donkey work and unnecessary if you have a food mill. The soup is not corn chowder, which would leave the kernels intact. It extracts the inner cornness from the kernels but preserves their memory, not only in flavor but in its garnish of whole kernels.

5 ears corn, shucked
5 cups milk
1 slice onion
5 tablespoons flour
Salt
White pepper
1 tablespoon butter

1. Cut the kernels away from the corn. Reserve.

2. Heat 4 cups of the milk with the onion slice in a 12-cup saucepan until foaming begins. Remove from the heat and discard the onion slice.

3. Add all the corn kernels except for ¼ cup. Return to the heat and simmer slowly for 10 minutes.

4. Run through a food mill, which should push the liquid and the corn mush through its sieve while retaining the kernel skins. Return the strained soup to the saucepan. Everything up to this point can be done the night before you plan to serve the soup. Refrigerate the soup until ready to use. Then bring to a very low simmer.

5. Whisk the flour into the remaining cup of milk. Add a cup of soup to the mixture and continue whisking until smooth. Pour into the soup. Continue simmering for 5 minutes. Season to taste with salt and white pepper.

6. Swirl the butter and reserved ¼ cup kernels into the soup and serve.

Serves 6

pastel de choclo
chilean corn pie

In Chile and Peru, corn kernels are large and translucent. Locals call this corn *choclo*. Small ear sections appear as a garnish for Peruvian ceviche. In Chile, this choclo "pie" is the national dish as well as Chile's sole contribution to world cuisine. If you can't find choclo, substitute normal corn but promise yourself that you'll snap up the first ears of choclo you run into in a Hispanic market and make the dish again while singing the Chilean national anthem.

½ pound ground beef

Salt and pepper

1 teaspoon ground cumin

1 garlic clove, peeled and finely chopped

2 tablespoons any vegetable oil except olive oil, approximately

½ cup raisins

6 ears Andean corn (choclo), about 4 cups corn kernels

1 cup whole milk

Butter for greasing the plates

2 medium onions, peeled and quartered

4 drumsticks or other pieces from a roasted chicken(s) or sautéed in oil for 20 minutes (optional)

8 pitted black olives

Sugar

1. Mix the ground beef together with salt and pepper to taste, the cumin, and the garlic. Let stand for an hour or two.

2. Heat the oil in a skillet and sauté the beef with the garlic and the raisins over medium heat for 10 minutes, until well browned. Reserve.

3. Meanwhile, strip the kernels from the ears of corn and process in bursts to produce a rough, uniform texture but not a finely milled meal. Stir together with the milk and simmer until the mixture thickens, stirring constantly. Reserve.

4. Preheat the oven to 300 degrees.

5. Butter the insides of four individual earthenware or other baking dishes.

6. Spread each dish with about one-eighth cup of the corn mixture. Then spread one-quarter of the ground-beef mixture. Arrange two of the onion quarters in each dish.

7. Place 1 piece of chicken, if you are using chicken, in the center of each dish. Add 2 olives. And cover everything with the remaining corn mixture. Sprinkle lightly with sugar and bake for 25 minutes. Raise the temperature to 400 degrees and bake another 15 minutes. Serve.

Serves 4

cress

Watercress is, as you have always thought, a cress that grows in watery places. I have seen it bent forward by the current of a fast-flowing stream in the Oxfordshire village of Ewhelme. Like you, I, too, have enjoyed its peppery tang, which reminds some people of mustard, another distant member of the enormous Cruciferae family. The scientific name, *Rorippa nasturtium-aquaticum*, alludes, as Davidson reminds us, to the "nose-twisting" quality of watercress implied by *nasturtium*, which means exactly that. Watercress is not at all related to the flower nasturtium. I have never tasted nasturtium blooms (or greens) and have no intention of doing so.

Watercress, and other closely related herbs, grow all over the world, often wild. Soup is their destiny in almost every culture that eats them. We in the West also eat them raw in salads and sandwiches. French* authorities claim they also prepare them like spinach and make purees of them bolstered by pureed potato or peas.

Davidson, in a memorable paragraph, collects notable examples of the use of watercress as a folk nostrum or medicinal: ". . . the Greek general made his soldiers eat it as a tonic. The Romans and Anglo-Saxons both ate it to avert baldness. Gerard (1633) recommended watercress as a remedy for that now forgotten disease 'greensickness of maidens.'† Francis Bacon advised that it would restore youth to ageing women; and so on."

---

*In the name of full disclosure I feel I must mention that the French word for watercress, *cresson*, has an adjective applied in formal menus to dishes containing said herb, viz., *à la cressonière*, very similar in form to the adjective for bush (*buisson/buissonière*), as in burning bush, *buis ardent*. To attend *l'école buissonière* is to play hooky, presumably by hiding in the bushes.

Edith Cresson, first woman premier of France (1991–1992), asserted publicly that one in four British men are homosexual and that the Japanese economy flourished because the Japanese were like ants.

†Also known as chlorosis, "a disease mostly affecting young females about the age of puberty, charac-terized by anæmia, suppression or irregularity of the menses, and a pale or greenish complexion; green sickness" (OED).

potage au cresson
watercress soup

2 pounds watercress

4 tablespoons butter

2 large potatoes, peeled and cut into eighths

3 cups water

Salt

2½ cups milk

2 cups heavy cream

3 egg yolks, lightly beaten

10 chervil sprigs

1. Rinse the watercress. Trim away the root ends, including the filamentous white parts. Reserve three dozen leaves in cold water. Rinse the remaining watercress a second time.

2. Melt the butter in a 6-cup saucepan. When the foam subsides, stir in the watercress. Lower the heat, cover, and stew for 10 to 15 minutes, until the cress has completely lost its turgor. Add the water, salt to taste, and the potatoes. Bring to a boil, cover, and simmer briskly for around 20 minutes, or until the potatoes give way when nudged.

3. Force through a food mill into a clean saucepan. Add the milk and bring to a boil. Lower the heat to low, add the reserved cress leaves (roughly chopped, if you like, to release their flavor), and simmer another 5 minutes.

4. Just before serving, whisk in the cream and the egg yolks off heat. Sprinkle with the chervil.

Serves 6

cucumbers

Cucumis sativus, the cultivated cucumber (literally, the Latin means the "sown cucumber")*, is a stealth vegetable, common worldwide, barely noticed anywhere. Mostly water, mild and grassy in taste, the cucumber can be and often is eaten raw. Anyone looking for a fresh vegetable in Germany will have gratefully discovered cucumber salad, *Gurkensalat,* an omnipresent first course on simple menus.

All three recipes are for uncooked cucumbers (unless you count the hot water bath for the pickles as cooking). The trick is to leach out as much of the water from them as possible (for the pickles, which are meant to be preserved without desiccation, the brine infiltrates the flesh and stabilizes it through the benign action of bacteria that can survive in a salty medium that suppresses the bad microbes, which would otherwise rot an untreated cuke).

Ever inconsistent, I will now reveal that my most exalted cucumber experience caught me by surprise in 1971 when I entered the kitchen of Helen McCully, a career "girl" (by then venerable but fleet of whisk and wit) and for many years food editor of *House Beautiful*. There stood Jacques Pépin, not yet a celebrated cookbook author and TV chef, sautéing cucumber slices in butter. With a snap of the wrist, he would periodically send the pale, skinned circles crashing against the back of the skillet. They would then rise, flip over obediently, and resume cooking on their other side. This was not only a great stunt but it made the water in the cucumbers vanish and replaced it with butter, unctuous and nutty.

*Many plants are officially denominated this way, viz., *Cannabis sativa*, the hemp plant aka marijuana, whose vernacular is, according to OED, an invention of English speakers who transformed the Mexican *mariguan* (itself possibly derived from Nahuatl *malliuan*, meaning prisoner [because it takes you prisoner??]) into a colloquial contraction of Maria Juana (a popular process of abbreviation yielding, all over the hispanophone world, names such as Marisol, Maricruz, Maricris, or, less obviously, Marisa (Maria Luisa), Maribel (Maria Isabel), and, not obviously at all, Concha (Maria Concepción).

cucumber sandwiches

No afternoon tea in England is ever without little cucumber sandwiches. Does this support the charge that the English are artless in the kitchen? Not at all. At teatime, only an oaf would demand veal Metternich or anything more substantial than a slice of cake. In the canonical tea menu, cucumber sandwiches have won pride of place with reason, as the gentle and genteel canape that suits the restrained and unpretentious tenor of the meal.

2 cucumbers, peeled and thinly sliced
2 tablespoons malt vinegar
Butter
10 slices white bread, crusts cut away

1. Put the cucumber slices in a bowl and pour the vinegar over them. Let stand for a half hour or more at room temperature, covered with a plate.
2. Butter the bread slices.
3. Drain the cucumber slices. Discard the liquid and arrange the cucumber on the buttered slices of bread. Cut them in quarters and serve. Be sure to pronounce cucumber as if it were spelled kookumber.

Serves 4 to 5

cacik/tzatziki/raita

In 1943, M.F.K. Fisher published *The Gastronomical Me*, a foodie's biography that tried as hard as it could to pretend the author wasn't a food snob. This trio of recipes for cucumber mixed with yogurt could be subtitled The Multicultural Me, because it shows off the same basic recipe as interpreted by Turks, Greeks, and Indians.

Cacık (pronounced *jajik*, really *jajök*, because the word is spelled in Turkish with a dotless *i* (ı) that sounds like an umlauted o in German: *Götterdämmerung*) is the ancestor, both phonologically and in fact, of the Greek *tzatziki*. Don't try out this idea in a taverna in Greek-controlled Cyprus, but almost everything Greeks put on the table is a legacy of Ottoman rule. Over time, however, things took their own Hellenic course, and tzatziki fits seamlessly into the Greek mini-cuisine of small plates of appetizers called *mezes*. Tzatziki is a dip, usually not tricked out with mint and dill, whereas cacik always has those herbs and often gets served as a soup. *Raita* is never served by itself. It is one of the many side dishes, breads, and condiments that accompany an Indian meal. And its seasonings—cumin, pepper, and cayenne—are typically Indian. So these are three distinct dishes, culturally distinct, gastronomically distinct, distinct in function and spirit. And yet, loath as I am to make cross-cultural comparisons, I do feel like saying the obvious: That three cultures—two still at each other's throats after many decades and the other having evolved far away from the other two at its own slowly simmering pace (albeit with a Middle Eastern influence from the Persian Mughals)—have embraced the same concept, as if any fool could see that cucumber and yogurt yearned to be mixed.*

2 cucumbers, peeled and grated

2 garlic cloves, finely chopped

2 tablespoons lemon juice or white vinegar

4 cups plain yogurt

½ teaspoon salt

¾ cup olive oil

¼ cup dill, chopped, and ¼ cup mint, chopped, or

    ½ teaspoon each cumin seeds, black pepper, and cayenne

*Like human beings, who, in the founding myth of sexuality that Diotima relates to the assembled revelers in Plato's *Symposium*, having originally been joined together in quadrupedal bliss, now bend their best efforts at regaining their former, coupled state.

1. Squeeze as much water as you can from the grated cucumber (unless you want to serve this as a cacik soup, in which case leave the water in. Stir the cucumber together with the garlic, the lemon juice or vinegar, the yogurt, the salt, and the olive oil.

2. For cacik, stir in the chopped dill and mint. For cacik soup, add water until you reach the desired consistency, about ⅔ cup. Chill.

3. For tzatziki, simply chill the mixture from step 1.

4. For raita, dry-roast the cumin seeds in an ungreased but tempered cast-iron kadhai or skillet over medium heat until the seeds darken. Grind them in a mortar or with a rolling pin. Add to the mixture from step 1 along with the black pepper and the cayenne. Chill.

Serves 6 to 8

dill pickles

A man once got up at a reading that I. B. Singer gave at the Young Men's Hebrew Association in New York and asked the great Yiddish writer's advice about dealing with a troublesome nephew. When the questioner subsided, Singer paused, looked at him with evident sympathy, and said: "I too have a nephew."

I think of that delicious moment as I am about to tell you about my grandma Mary's dill pickles. I can hear you thinking: I too have a grandma who made incomparable (fill in the blank). But it is true that my grandmother made incomparable sour dill pickles and some awfully good dill tomatoes as well. She put them up in the fall in Mason jars, nobbly pickles* that sat in her dark cellar (the same cellar where my grandfather's library of Yiddish books he'd bound himself got ruined in a basement flood long after his death) all winter.

Grandma Mary tended to overdo it. She sent us off with so many jars that we never could finish them. They became a kind of joke, but I don't laugh anymore when I buy mass-produced pickles. Next year, I will, for my own sake and, *pietatis causa*, put up my own pickles. What could it hurt?

1 cup kosher salt

2 cups cider vinegar

8 fresh dill sprigs

8 garlic cloves, peeled and chopped

Four 1-quart glass Mason jars and lids, sterilized in boiling water for 10 minutes
    (do not boil the flat vacuum disks)

2 pounds Kirby cucumbers, no longer than 4 inches

1. Bring 6 cups of water to a boil with the salt and the vinegar.

2. Put 2 of the dill sprigs and one-quarter of the chopped garlic in each jar. Then pack them as full as possible with the cucumbers.

3. Pour the boiling brine over the cucumbers, leaving an inch or so of air at the top. Seal the jars.

4. Bring the water used to sterilize the jars back to a boil. Put the filled jars back in the water. They should be completely covered with water with a couple inches to spare. Simmer for 15 minutes. Remove from the hot water and let cool. The contraction of cooling will pull the lids airtight. Both the sterilization and this step are much easier to do with a canner—a large pot with a jar rack that fits inside it—and a jar lifter. The rack makes it more convenient and safer to lower several jars into hot water. The jar lifter is, duh, for lifting the hot jars out of hot water.

5. Store the pickles at room temperature for a month before tasting. If they are not sour enough, store them 2 weeks longer. Taste again.

Makes 4 quarts sour, garlic dill pickles

*The cucumber variety known as Kirbys. The erudite Elizabeth Schneider, in *Vegetables from Amaranth to Zucchini* (2001), states that true Kirbys disappeared from the market in the mid-1930s. A cucumber sometimes called Kirby Stays Green was introduced, she says, "in 1920 by I. N. Simon & Son in Philadelphia and registered under the name of its developer, Norval E. Kirby, a company employee." Kirbys did not stay green, in fact, but withered away from disease, cuke palsy or some such. The name, however, survives as a catchall for smallish, nobbly, pickling-type cucumbers.

eggplant

E ggplant, *Solanum melongena*, a member of the Solanaceae family, like the tomato, the potato, and the deadly nightshade, originated in India. So it must have reached the Middle East through contact between Islamic and Indic cultures. The obvious vector for the eggplant diaspora was the Mughal (Persian) conquest of India in 1526, which connected India with the rest of the Muslim world. The ensuing migration of eggplant westward with the Arabs across Africa to Spain can be tracked linguistically, beginning with Hindi *brinjal*, evolving naturally into Arabic *al-berenjena*, which produced *aubergine* (French and then British English), *berenjena* (Spanish), and *melanzana* (Italian).

And "eggplant"? Perhaps you have seen the small, almost circular eggplants sometimes for sale in farm markets or specialty grocers. Such eggplants likely inspired the botanist whom OED quotes as having written in 1794: "When this [its fruit] is white it has the name of Egg-Plant."

Curiously, "aubergine" first appeared in English in the same year, in a treatise on Surinam, assuming OED has the goods here. The same entry stumbles badly in its eurocentric etymology: "[Fr., dim. of auberge, variant of alberge 'a kind of peach' (Littré), ad. Sp. alberchigo, alverchiga, 'an apricocke' (Minsheu 1623)]."

baba ghannooge
lebanese eggplant puree

Roasting eggplant over an open flame is essential to the proper smoky flavor of the ultimate puree. Spongy eggplant flesh absorbs the flavor and the oil of the tahini, that sesame-seed paste typical of Arab cooking. The result is one of those great prescientific human discoveries we owe to experimental cooks who took what they could from plundering armies. The advancing Arabs brought eggplant from the East, then some genius realized that eggplant would meld perfectly with another unlikely edible product of proto-industrial ingenuity, an oily paste ground from sesame seeds.

4 large eggplants
¼ cup tahini
3 garlic cloves, peeled and mashed
Juice of 2 small lemons
Salt
Fresh mint leaves or parsley leaves or paprika or pomegranate seeds
Olive oil

1. Score the eggplants all over to prevent bursting during cooking. Stick a long barbecue fork into the round (nonstem end) and roast over an open wood or charcoal fire (or over a gas burner), turning frequently until they collapse internally and are nicely charred outside. Don't overdo the charring, even though, in moderation, it adds an essential smoky taste to the eggplant puree. You can bake the eggplants in a 350-degree oven, but why bother? While this method will produce the same texture as the others, it will not provide the right taste.

2. Pull away the stems and skin as soon as you can touch them. Put the flesh in a colander and let it drain for 15 minutes. This legendarily allows potentially bitter liquid to drain away, but its actual benefit, aside from masking the bitter taste that some eggplants still have despite yeoman efforts by plantsmen, is to draw water out of the cells into the spongy air pockets that would otherwise take up too much oil from the tahini.

3. Mash the flesh in a wooden bowl, using a fork or a potato masher, working along the grain of the pulp (from stem to stern). You can also puree the eggplant by pulsing two or three times in a processor, but the texture will be smoother, and therefore less interesting, than the hand-mashed puree.

4. Stir in the tahini, the mashed garlic, the lemon juice, and the salt to taste.

5. Transfer the puree to a dinner plate or other shallow serving dish. Spread it smoothly with a slightly thicker amount around the edge.

6. Decorate the center of the puree with a star* of mint or parsley leaves or paprika or pomegranate seeds. If you pick pomegranate seeds, the most dazzling option, then tradition and Anissa Helou dictate that you sprinkle paprika over the raised outer edge of the puree. Finally, dribble rays of olive oil from the periphery to the decorated center. Serve with pita wedges.

Serves 6

---

*Anissa Helou does not specify what kind of star, but I don't suppose she means a star of David.

eggplant imam bayildi

This is the most famous of all eggplant dishes. It is also the only recipe of any kind whose name is a sentence. *Imam bayıldı* means "The imam fainted." The traditional explanation for it is that some imam fainted from pleasure when he tasted this oil-drenched eggplant concoction. To a turcophone reader, there is nothing odd about the verb *bayıldı*, the third-person singular preterite of the verb "to faint": *bayılmak*. But to non-Turks, especially those wanting to spell *bayıldı* correctly (and wouldn't it be embarrassing to quote something from Turkish without spelling it correctly?), the crucial point is that the letter that looks like an *i* is not an *i* but a dotless *ı*, written *ı* (in this font, it is identical with a small numeral one) and pronounced like the German *ö* or *oe* as in *Föhn** or Goethe.[†]

2 medium eggplants

Oil (preferably olive oil)

1 medium onion, peeled and finely chopped

1 medium tomato, chopped

Salt

Pepper

¼ teaspoon allspice

½ teaspoon chopped parsley

1 tablespoon currants, soaked in cold water for 30 minutes

1 garlic clove, peeled

I bay leaf

1. Cut the stems off the eggplants but do not peel. Cut several lengthwise slits in the eggplants but do not slice through.

*The mountain wind that grows warmer as it descends the Alps, especially in southern Germany. This "Föhn effect" occurs elsewhere under many local names: Zonda in Argentina, as found in Aconcagua Provincial park; the Puelche, also in the Andes; the Halny Wiatr in Poland; the Koembang in Java; the Santa Ana in California; the Chinook in the Rocky Mountains; the Sirocco in North Africa, Greece, and Spain; the Harmattan in West Africa; the Bora in the former Yugoslavia; the Simoom in Arabia; the Kamsin in Syria; and the Samiel in Turkey.

[†]Johann Wolfgang von Goethe (1749–1832), poet and polymath. His pan-European fame reached as far as Detroit, where the street named after him is pronounced Go-thee, as in theme.

2. Heat 2 tablespoons olive oil in a small skillet and sauté the onion until it browns lightly. Then add the tomato, salt, pepper, allspice, and parsley. Cook over medium-low heat until the mixture breaks down almost into a puree.

3. Drain the currants, add them to the tomato-onion mixture, and cook for 10 more minutes. Let cool.

4. Stuff the cooked mixture in the slits in the eggplants with your fingers or a knife.

5. Set the eggplants in a flameproof dish that will just hold them. Pour oil over the eggplants until the oil level is about halfway up them. Add the garlic and bay leaf to the oil.

6. Cover the dish and cook over very low heat for an hour, or until the eggplants are very soft. Turn them every 15 minutes. When they are done, pour off the excess oil and strain and store it for reuse. Cool and refrigerate the eggplants overnight. Serve them cold in thin slices.

Serves 6 as an appetizer or side dish

moussaka
eggplant baked with ground lamb

Even the most chauvinist of Greek authors concede that this casserole of eggplant (*Solanum melongena* L.) and ground meat came to them (as did so much else) with the Ottoman occupation. Evidence on the ground supports this: Moussaka without the white-sauce topping prevalent in Greece is eaten throughout the Middle East, and called "moussaka." And it is hard to see how such a dish would have spread from Greece to the rest of the Turkish empire and then become simplified. In any case, "moussaka" is not a Greek word. The Turks brought "moussaka" to Athens from Egypt, where it is colloquial for "chilled." Perhaps it was originally eaten cold. There is no fixed recipe. The full-dress Greek version can be respectably produced with lamb or beef or even veal, but lamb would seem to be the inevitable choice for a Middle Eastern dish. When did Greeks add tomatoes? Almost certainly after they had learned to make moussaka. Purists can simply eliminate the tomato, just as they can opt (as I have) for a yogurt-based white sauce. Then there is the matter of how to parcook the eggplant slices: fry or grill? Claudia Roden says grilled slices are lighter, but are they more delicious? She says yes; I disagree, but the huge amount of oil that eggplant absorbs in frying makes me line up with Ms. Roden.

That moussaka, so deeply rooted in the Islamic Middle East, should be known as Greek in the Christian West, is a small sign of the way Greece and the Balkans have served as a point of entry for a multifarious family of cuisines that merged during the Ottoman centuries but which are fundamentally either Turkish or fused with Turkish food. This is the culinary side of an ironic fairy tale in which the culturally unoriginal Greeks of the post-Byzantine period have come to enjoy an unearned prestige in Europe, because of an ancient Greek civilization whose language they can no longer read and a cuisine they picked up from their Turkish masters.

2 pounds eggplant, unpeeled but trimmed and cut in rounds about ½ inch thick

Salt

3 tablespoons oil

1 large onion, peeled and chopped

1½ pounds ground lamb

½ cup tomato puree

2 teaspoons ground cinnamon

2 teaspoons sugar

Pepper

3 tablespoons finely chopped flat-leaf parsley

2 cups plain whole milk yogurt

3 eggs, lightly beaten

¾ cup grated cheese (Gruyère, Cheddar, or kefalotyri)

Grated nutmeg

1. Put the eggplant slices in a large colander. Toss them in salt and let stand for at least a half hour.

2. Heat the oil in a large skillet. Brown the onion with the lamb. Stir in the tomato puree, cinnamon, sugar, and pepper to taste. Lower the heat and continue cooking until all the liquid evaporates. Stir in the parsley and let cool.

3. Rinse the eggplant slices; pat dry with a paper towel.

4. Grill or broil the eggplant slices until they are lightly browned.

5. Preheat the oven to 375 degrees.

6. In a bowl, whisk together all the remaining ingredients and season with salt and pepper.

7. Lightly oil the inside of a 10 by 14-inch ovenproof dish. Cover the bottom with a layer of half the eggplant slices. Then spread on it a layer of all the lamb mixture. Finally add the rest of the eggplant in an even layer. Pour the yogurt mixture over the top and bake in the oven for about 45 minutes, until golden brown on top.

Serves 6 to 8

ratatouille

This medley of three Solanaceae (two New World—tomatoes and red peppers—one Old World—eggplant) plus zucchini was historically possible only after 1492, but the mixture has coalesced in the minds of everyone except food-history pedants into an emblematic dish of Provence.

6 large red bell peppers, prepared as in steps 1 and 2 on page 96
1⅓ cups olive oil
1¾ pounds onions, peeled and thinly sliced
1½ pounds zucchini, roughly diced
1 head garlic
2 pounds eggplant, stem removed and roughly diced, with skin left on
2 pounds tomatoes, blanched, skinned, seeded, and cut into large chunks
5 thyme sprigs
Salt and pepper

1. Cut the bell peppers into long thin strips. Set aside with their liquid.

2. Heat ⅓ cup of the olive oil in a Dutch oven over very low heat. Stir in the sliced onions, cover, and cook for about a half hour, or until they are completely softened and breaking down. Stir occasionally.

3. Uncover, raise the heat a bit, and continue cooking until the onions turn a light brown. Stir in the zucchini and the garlic head. Continue cooking and stir occasionally.

4. Meanwhile, heat the rest of the olive oil over medium-high heat in a large skillet. Dump in the eggplant and sauté until softened. With a slotted spoon, transfer to the large pot and stir into the zucchini mixture. Continue cooking and stirring the large pot, while you sauté the tomatoes in the oil left in the skillet until they reduce to a thick mass. Scrape them with any remaining liquid into the large pot.

5. Add the reserved red peppers and their liquid along with the thyme sprigs and salt and pepper to taste. Cook over low heat, stirring occasionally, for another hour, or as long as it takes to boil away most of the liquid.

6. Fish out the garlic head with a slotted spoon. Mash through the strainer, leaving the skin and stem behind, back into the pot. Stir all the ingredients together and correct the seasoning.

7. Let the ratatouille cool in a serving dish. Cover and refrigerate for a day or two if you can. The flavor improves. Serve hot or at room temperature.

Serves 8 to 10

endives

Endive is chicory and chicory is endive (unless it is radicchio), although they are not the same. How can this be? The confusion is purely nomenclatural, or you could blame it on the Belgians. Around 1850, plantsmen at the Brussels botanic garden decided to force the roots of *Cichorium intybus*, up till then mainly exploited as a coffee ersatz, to grow leaves indoors in darkness. Buried under soil, to encourage a tight head of leaves, the plant complied and the leaves themselves came up out of the ground all pale and mildly bitter.

The same plant, but with red and white leaves, is called radicchio. It is normally seen in a round, tightly headed form. Another variety of radicchio, called Treviso, has long, loosely headed leaves with an underhue of green.

The center of production in Europe continues to be Brussels, where French-speaking Walloons call this unnatural sprout *chicon* and Flemings refer to it as *witloof*, or white leaf. They order things differently in France, of course, where the same vegetable is *endive* or *chicorée*. In the U.K., markets sell it as Belgian or Brussels chicory. In the U.S., we have settled for Belgian endive.

You'll know it when you see it. Eating it raw with Gorgonzola and walnuts is my favorite way to serve it. Braising in a moderate oven in a greased gratin pan with a little chicken stock is a simple and excellent way to go if you want to cook it. The recipe below is a classic Belgian dish, one you will find almost anywhere in Brussels.

While the witloof bakes, you'll have time to make a chicory salad from true endive (*Cichorium endivia*), either from the curly type (aka curly chicory or frisée) or from the broad-leaf variety (aka escarole). Should you wish to cook this plant, either variety can be sautéed or steamed until wilted. The final recipe is a variation on a basic Italian soup combo, escarole and starch (rice, pasta, or beans).

chicons au gratin
belgian endives au gratin

In an embellished version of this dish, the endives are wrapped in ham at the end of step 2. Many recipes call for prosciutto, but why not preserve the regional spirit of the dish and look for a ham from the Ardennes, the region straddling the French-Belgian border famous also as the site of the Battle of the Bulge* and the birthplace of Rimbaud at Charleville.[†]

6 tablespoons butter, approximately

8 endives, with root ends trimmed away

2 tablespoons flour

1¼ cups milk

½ cup heavy cream

½ cup grated Gruyère cheese

Salt

White pepper

½ cup dried bread crumbs

1. Preheat the oven to 375 degrees.

2. Butter the bottom and sides of a gratin dish or other ovenproof dish just large enough to hold the endives in a single layer. Arrange the endives in it.

3. Melt 2 tablespoons of the butter in a small, heavy skillet over low heat. When the foam subsides, whisk in the flour and continue whisking for 3 minutes. Whisk in the milk and cream. Continue cooking and whisking until this béchamel sauce has thickened. Remove from the heat and whisk in the cheese, salt, and pepper.

4. Pour the sauce over the endives. Sprinkle with the bread crumbs.

5. Melt 2 tablespoons butter and pour over the bread crumbs.

6. Bake for 30 minutes, or until the bread crumbs are a golden brown. Serve immediately.

Serves 4

*This was the final great battle of World War II, which began on December, 16, 1944, and ended January 25, 1945. The bloody encounter culminated at Bastogne in Belgium near the German border.

[†]Arthur Rimbaud (1854–1891), prodigal, decadent poet, lashed out in his early works at the provincial world he was born into and soon escaped to a far worse place, the Arabian desert.

grilled radicchio

Radicchio was completely unavailable in the U.S. until in the early 1980s. When it did appear, it was very expensive, unless you could persuade a mystified checkout clerk that it was red cabbage. Grilling slightly reduces the bitterness of the leaves and, of course, softens them.

6 medium heads radicchio

Olive oil

Salt

Pepper

1. Slice the radicchio heads in half lengthwise. Cut out and discard the solid white part at the base as well as any discolored leaves.

2. Lightly oil a shallow ovenproof dish that will just contain the sliced radicchio in a single layer. Arrange them cut side down.

3. Fifteen minutes before you are ready to serve them, preheat the broiler.

4. Set the dish on a rack at the oven's highest level and broil for 3 to 4 minutes, or until the radicchio halves are barely softened and nicely colored but not blackened. Add the salt and pepper to taste. Turn them once halfway through. Of course, you can also do this by grilling the pieces directly over charcoal. Or you could braise them in a 350-degree oven for 10 to 15 minutes, covered in aluminum foil. Serve hot or cold.

Serves 6

zuppa di scarola e peperoni
escarole soup with peppers

¼ cup olive oil

2 garlic cloves, peeled and thinly sliced

2 pounds escarole, trimmed, washed, and cut in diagonal 2-inch-wide strips

6 cups chicken stock

2 medium bell peppers

1 green chile

¼ pound ditalini*

Salt

1. Heat 2 tablespoons of the olive oil in a 6-quart saucepan. Toss in half of the sliced garlic cloves. When the garlic browns, add the escarole slices and stir-fry until wilted.

2. Add the stock, bring to a boil, lower the heat, and simmer for 20 minutes, covered.

3. Meanwhile, stem and seed the two peppers and the chile. Cut in very thin slices and reserve.

4. Heat the remaining 2 tablespoons olive oil in a medium skillet. Toss in the remaining garlic and brown. Then add the peppers and chile slices. Sauté until softened.

5. Add the ditalini to the soup and simmer for 5 minutes, or until al dente. Pour into soup bowls and garnish with the peppers.

Serves 4

*Literally "thimbles," these short, unridged segments of tube pasta are slightly curved and open at both ends but look as though they could be slid over a finger.

fennel

Fennel is a quadruple threat, or perhaps it would be more accurate to call it a quadruple treat. The feathery leaves make a nice, dill-like addition to fish dishes. The stalks contribute the same anise flavor when fish is roasted over them, as in the French dish *loup au fenouil* (sea bass with fennel). The seeds first appear as yellow blossoms in the umbrellalike spray that marks this plant as a member of the Umbelliferae family (along with carrots and many other vegetables and spices)*. But it is the swollen, bulbous leaf base of the variety known as Florence fennel that has made this versatile plant the favorite vegetable of Italy.

The species name, *Foeniculum*, is a diminutive of the Latin for hay (*faenum*, *foenum*, or *fenum*). The full Linnaean appellation is *F. vulgare* var. *azoricum*. This implies that Florence fennel (itself almost certainly a Briticism reflecting the gastronomic encounter of a botanizing English epicure on the Grand Tour in Italy), a plant known to antiquity, was considered by some modern taxonomist to have originated in the mid-Atlantic on the now-Portuguese islands of the Azores.

In Italy, fennel is *finocchio*, which is also slang for homosexual, because it is a contraction for "dainty eye," *fino occhio*. In ancient Greek, fennel was "marathon" (μάραθον, or outside Attica, the region that includes Athens, marathron, μάραθρον). The ancient traveler Strabo[†] believed that the town of Marathon, famous as a fifth-century B.C. battlesite and a footrace,[‡] got its name because it was rife with fennel. The name persists in all senses, geographic, botanic, and athletic, in modern Greece (μάραθον, or μάραθρον).

The combination of celerylike crunch and aniselike taste makes fennel appealing to eat raw in salads or in the classic Roman snack below. When sautéed or steamed, fennel bulbs, having lost some of their anise flavor, accompany almost any main course with verve.

---

[*]Celery, parsnips, anise, caraway, chervil, coriander, cumin, and dill.

[†]Strabo wrote in Greek but lived in a world increasingly dominated by Roman imperial power (born c. 63 B.C., died after A.D. 21). His name means "squinter" in Greek and Latin. In modern medical parlance, strabismus, or strabism, refers to chronic squinting. In the 1960s, Strabo Vivian Clagett III wrote a fight song for Harvard College and submitted it to the *Crimson*, the undergraduate daily. Never officially adopted, it is now lost.

[‡]The battle took place approximately twenty-five miles from Athens on the plain of Marathon in September 490 B.C. Deploying his outnumbered troops with mastery (in the account given by Herodotus), the Athenian general Miltiades routed the invading Persians led by Darius I and thereby saved Greece from "barbarian" (non–Greek-speaking) domination.

This victory allowed Athens to flourish and produce most of the greatest works of Greek literature—tragedies, comedy, lyric poetry, and philosophy—the bedrock of what became Western culture.

As to the story of the footrace, Herodotus tells us of the runner Pheidippides, but says only that he ran to Sparta pleading for help. Much later, Plutarch (c. A.D. 25–145) set down the probably invented tale of Pheidippides's run from Marathon to Athens with news of the victory.

cuori di finocchio in pinzimonio
marinated fennel hearts

2 fennels
¼ cup olive oil
Salt
Pepper

1. Cut off the tops of the fennels, leaving just the bulbs. Remove the outer leaves and discard. Cut a slice off the bottoms. Then cut the bulbs in quarters and dry them.
2. Put the olive oil in a bowl and season abundantly with salt and pepper. This is the pinzimonio.
3. Dip pieces of fennel in the pinzimonio and eat them out of hand. This Roman delicacy can also be prepared with hearts of celery.

Serves 4

kale

ribollita
tuscan "reboiled" bean and greens soup

In the food counterculture, the well-heeled cabal that militates against fast food and overprecious chefs, Frankenfoods and pesticides, and antibiotically treated meat, *ribollita* is the poster dish. What more could Slow Foodies ask for than a peasant soup "reboiled" from yesterday's leftovers? Devotees of *cucina povera*, the cooking of the poor, could hardly invent anything "poorer" than this celebrated and adored member of a whole, hearty Italian family of "poor" soups and peasant *minestre*. And there is the added touch of poignance that this is a Tuscan peasant soup, now that rural Tuscany is mostly populated by expatriate Germans and by Brits who jokingly call it Chiantishire.

Far be it from me, however, to vie with my betters over who is more down to earth. I like a peasant soup as much as the next college graduate, and ribollita is a great peasant soup, but it has inspired the kind of dogfight over authenticity among its nonpeasant fans that peasant food so often does.

After all, the point of getting back to a preindustrial, uncontaminated style of eating has to be that we decadent urbanites can find a path back to a Rousseauian simplicity, to a real, viz., an authentic, country table. No microwaves need apply. And the ingredients must be precisely the ingredients traditionally used for each dish in the age of horsedrawn plows.

If you scan the list of ingredients below, you will be struck by one item that you didn't grow up with in Akron. *Cavolo nero*, literally "black cabbage," is the equivalent for this recipe of what mountain climbers call the crux of a climb, the one place on a pitch that has to be overcome if you are going to succeed in moving upward to the next pitch or finish the ascent. Put simply, no cavolo nero, no ribollita.

I had been told by dyed-in the-homespun ribollitistas practicing their religion in Manhattan that cavolo nero was unavailable on this side of the Atlantic. I'd have to rent a villa in Radda in Chianti near them if I wanted to make ribollita myself. Then I opened Benedetta Vitali's *Soffritto, Tradition and Innovation in Tuscan Cooking* (2001) and discovered that cavolo nero was actually sold in the New World as elephant kale or lacinato kale.

Although Ms. Vitali is a real Tuscan and runs a restaurant in Florence, she took the trouble to find out how American readers could find what they needed to duplicate her food. No longer did I have to decide whether to cross the Atlantic or make do with ordinary kale if I was going to purify my toxic soul with ribollita.

But don't get me wrong, I will be happy to make this soup with the traditional crux (and cruciferous) ingredient, but I've tried it with kale and even plain green cabbage, and the idea was strong enough to survive the substitution. This is life in the big city. Get used to it. But eat more ribollita.

2½ cups dried cannellini beans

5 garlic cloves, peeled and minced

5 sage leaves

2½ cups olive oil, approximately

2 onions, peeled and chopped fine

5 carrots, peeled and chopped fine

3 celery stalks, trimmed and chopped fine

5 potatoes, peeled and chopped fine

3 zucchini, peeled and chopped fine

½ Savoy cabbage, cut as for slaw

10 leaves cavolo nero (black cabbage sold as elephant kale or lacinato kale) or ordinary kale*

6 leeks, trimmed, carefully rinsed, and sliced (green and white parts)

6 cups beef stock

4 thyme sprigs

Salt, if needed

Tuscan or other sourdough bread, sliced about ½ inch thick

1. Soak the beans overnight in enough cold water to cover them by 2 inches. The next day add 2 garlic cloves and the sage. Bring to a boil and simmer very slowly, covered, for about an hour. Do not stir. The beans are done when they are just tender. Reserve with the cooking liquid.

2. Heat ¾ cup of the olive oil in a skillet and sauté the onions, carrots, and celery until lightly browned. Then add the potatoes, zucchini, cabbage, cavolo nero or kale, leeks, remaining garlic, and the beans with their liquid. Add the beef stock to cover and the thyme.

3. Bring to a boil, reduce the heat, and simmer gently for about a half hour.

*For the record, kale is a cabbage without a head. The scientific name states this clearly: *Brassica oleracea* var. *acephala. B. oleracea*, the species name, includes a superficially diverse group of plants ranging from cabbage-patch cabbage to Chinese kale to cauliflower to Brussels sprouts to kohlrabi, nonsprouting and sprouting broccoli (calabrese) to curly kale. Clearly, the human hand has been long at work exploiting the genes of the wild cabbage, *B. oleracea* var. *oleracea,* which itself resembles kale. This suggests that kale was the original cultivar. This long history may explain why there are so many varieties of kale quite distinct from other varieties of *B. oleracea* var. *acephala.* Collards, for example, are a heat-tolerant type of kale popular in the U.S. South. Ornamental kales are multicolored and, despite being nominally acephalous, form loose heads.

4. Stir in the remaining oil. Add salt if necessary.

5. In a clean pot you can serve the soup from, pour in an inch of soup. Cover with a layer of bread slices. Alternate layers of soup and bread until the soup is used up. Finish with a layer of bread. Then add additional beef stock to saturate the bread.

6. Let rest for several hours. Before serving, reheat over low heat, stirring gently.

Serves 10

leeks

Until the last ten years or so, it was a rare pleasure to find leeks in a U.S. market. Although they belong to the same genus, *Allium*, as onions, shallots, and scallions (all three of them varieties of *A. cepa*); garlic (*A. sativa*) and chives, both ordinary and Chinese (*A. schoenoprasum* and *A. tuberosum*, respectively); leeks (*A. porrum*) are distinct in their mildness and subtlety of flavor. It is true that ordinary onions can be broiled and served whole, as can pearl onions. Even garlic heads can be roasted or stewed in their entirety and then eaten. But leeks are the epicure's choice among the alliums, mild and subtly flavored. They used to require extensive washing to remove the sand that had infiltrated their tightly packed layers during growth. But the leeks I find now are very clean, although I still check them carefully.

Leeks are also funny. They are a favorite joke vegetable for Aristophanes, most notably at *Frogs* 621. Aeacus lists several horrible punishments that Xanthias should inflict on him if he catches him in a crime: whipping, hanging, pouring vinegar into his nose. "But don't smack me with a leek or a spring onion."

Agatha Christie winked at her readers when she named her Belgian detective Hercule Poirot, a small and dandy fellow incongruously identified with the mythical strongman and a humble vegetable (poirot = *poireau* = leek).

The leek found its warmest welcome in Wales, where it is the symbol of Welsh nationalism, raised on flagpoles on St. David's Day, March 1. David, or Dewi in Welsh, lived in the sixth century. According to his biographer, Righyfarch, he drank only water (Dewi Ddyfrwr = David the Waterbibber) and sometimes mortified his flesh by immersing himself to the neck in icy waters while reciting Holy Writ. He was a vegetarian, too, at a time when leeks were a major part of the Welsh diet. On top of that, David's contemporary, King Cadwallader, ordered his troops to attach leeks to their helmets before they fought the Saxons. This prevented deaths from friendly fire (the tale assumes that the Saxons did not also don leek nosegays), and since the Welsh won, they ever after clung to the leek as their emblem. Along the way, the daffodil also became a Welsh national symbol. According to one source, both leek and daffodil have the same name in Welsh, *ceninen*. Can this be true? Or is it a backhanded swipe at the Welsh (not as crude as the ditty "Taffy is a Welshman, Taffy is a Thief. . . . ," but still), implying that they can't tell the difference between a leek and a daffodil. Shakespeare himself makes sport of the Welsh and their leekiness in *Henry V*, V.1.1–34, a scene full of leek-based phallic persiflage aimed at the Welshman Fluellen.

braised leeks

This can also be done on the top of the stove over low-medium heat, but the oven method requires less attention. Either way, with very little trouble, you get the most classic leek dish: long, soft, pale-yellow, still-intact cylinders, slightly collapsed, surprisingly tasty. Cut with steak knives to avoid tearing.

12 medium leeks
1 cup chicken stock, approximately
2 tablespoons butter
Salt
White pepper
1 cup white wine

1. Trim away the root ends and the green sections from the leeks. Discard. Wash the leeks well in cold water. Then make an X in the root end of each leek. Spread them open. Wash out any sand.

2. Preheat the oven to 350 degrees.

3. Pack the leeks tightly in the bottom of an ovenproof pot. Pour the stock over them. It should come about halfway up the leeks. Dot with butter. Add salt and white pepper to taste. Bring the stock to a boil, cover, and set in the oven for 15 minutes, or until the leeks have completely lost their turgor.

4. With tongs, remove the leeks to a serving platter.

5. Add the wine to the cooking liquid and reduce to 1 cup. Pour over the leeks and serve.

Serves 6

vichyssoise

Despite the name, this is not a regional dish from Vichy but an American turn on leek-and-potato soup.

6 leeks, trimmed and rinsed as for Braised Leeks (page 136)
4 tablespoons butter
8 large potatoes, peeled and quartered
12 cups chicken stock (optional)
Salt
White pepper
¾ cup heavy cream
2 tablespoons chopped chives

1. Slice the leeks in thin rounds.

2. Heat the butter in a Dutch oven until it melts and the foam subsides. Stir in the leeks. Lower the heat, cover, and simmer until the leeks and onion are translucent.

3. Add the potatoes, the chicken stock (for Vichyssoise) or water (for French leek-and-potato soup), and the salt and white pepper to taste. Bring to a boil, lower the heat, and simmer, uncovered, for a half hour, or until the potatoes are soft. Mash them with a fork. At this point, you have a traditional French leek-and-potato soup. Serve it hot.

4. For Vichyssoise, let the soup cool, process in batches, and then stir in the heavy cream. Scatter the chives on top of the soup and serve.

Serves 8 to 10

lentils

The lesson for today comes from the twenty-fifth chapter of Genesis, lines 29–34:

> And Jacob sod* pottage: and Esau came from the field, and he was faint:
>
> And Esau said to Jacob, Feed me, I pray thee, with that same red pottage; for I am faint: therefore was his name called Edom.†
>
> And Jacob said, Sell me this day thy birthright.
>
> And Esau said, Behold, I am at the point to die: and what profit shall this birthright do to me?
>
> And Jacob said, Swear to me this day; and he sware unto him: and he sold his birthright unto Jacob.
>
> Then Jacob gave Esau bread and pottage of lentiles; and he did eat and drink, and rose up, and went his way: thus Esau despised his birthright.

masoor dal 140

So lentil soup is one of the oldest recorded dishes. Herodotus mentions lentils as a crop from the exotic north (4.17.1). Modern cultures from Argentina to India eat these little seeds in enormous quantity, more than a million tons a year. They come in many colors: brown, yellow, orange. And at some point they gave their Latin name, *lens*, to the lens we see through, whether in the eye or in front of it. This is not merely an etymological curiosity but a living fact in modern life. The same word refers to the pulse and the optical disk in French (*lentille*), Italian (*lènte*), Spanish (*lenteja*), and German (*Linse*).

Depending on how one first came upon this word in France, say, it comes as a jolt to discover that *lentilles de contacte* are contact lenses and not some invention of a chef. Or, conversely, in Germany, that *Linse* are something you put in your mouth and not in your eyes.

I love to slice up an onion and add it to a package of lentils that have been soaking in water along with salt and a kielbasa cut in rounds. This is indeed what Mother used to call a meal in itself.

I also like nothing better than that French farmhouse standby *cou d'oie farci aux lentilles* (stuffed goose neck with lentils). I would prepare it regularly if I had easy access to goose necks.

For us, for our family, and for Americans in general, lentils are not a central element of the daily diet, even though they are 25 percent protein and laughably cheap. Indians, on the other hand, consume them at most meals, as a side dish called *dal*. Dal is, for lack of a better word, a porridge made from dried lentils, beans, peas, or chickpeas. Some dals are soupy, while at the other extreme are dals in which the lentils or beans retain their shape. Masoor dal is a split lentil with a pink or salmon color. In the recipe below, you will not bring down the wrath of Shiva on your head if you substitute yellow or brown lentils.

*Archaic past tense of seethe, to soak or boil

†Red

masoor dal

2 cups split pink lentils, washed and soaked for 30 minutes

¾ teaspoon fenugreek seeds

2 green chiles (serrano), trimmed, seeded, and chopped fine

¼ cup any vegetable oil, except olive oil or ghee

1 teaspoon mustard seeds

1 teaspoon cumin seeds

½ teaspoon asafetida

2 garlic cloves, crushed and peeled

1 large tomato, chopped

2 to 3 teaspoons cayenne

½ teaspoon turmeric

½ teaspoon ground coriander

½ teaspoon ground cumin

½ teaspoon garam masala

Salt

Juice of 1 lemon

2 tablespoons chopped coriander leaves (cilantro)

1. Bring 8 cups of water to a boil in a Dutch oven.

2. Add the lentils, the fenugreek seeds, and the chopped green chiles. Lower the heat, cover, and simmer for 45 minutes, or until the lentils are soft.

3. Heat the oil or ghee in a skillet. Add the mustard seeds, the cumin seeds, and the asafetida. Cook until the seeds begin to pop. Then stir in the crushed garlic, the chopped tomato, the five ground spices (cayenne, turmeric, coriander, cumin, and garam masala), the salt to taste, and ¼ cup water. Stir-fry just long enough to mix all the ingredients and heat them. Scrape into the dal pot. Bring to a boil, stirring. Lower the heat, cover, and simmer for 3 minutes.

4. Remove from the heat. Stir in the lemon juice and then the coriander leaves.

Serves 8

lettuce

The history of lettuce is not full of incident. Marco Polo did not bring back lettuce to Europe from Cathay (any more than he legendarily exported pasta). Marie Antoinette did not tell Parisians short on bread to eat lettuce instead. Although lettuce was certainly known to the Romans of Petronius's day, it does not figure in the menu alongside honeyed dormice* at the banquet of Trimalchio in his *Satyricon*. But lettuce is not boring. Cultigens of *Lactuca*† *sativa* run the visual and physical gamut from bitter to peppery, green to red, tightly headed to loose-leafed, flat to curly. Needless to say, everyone knows about lettuce.

Still, there are a few recondite lettucisms a gastrotrivialist could dine out on. Wild lettuce (*L. serriola*) is a mild soporific. In ancient days it was considered a medicinal.

Cultivated varieties will not give you a buzz unless you consume a desperate quantity. Our lettuces have had the downer bred out of them along with a lot of the wild-type bitterness.

You can cook lettuce by braising. But obviously the overwhelmingly most common form of lettuce consumption outside Asia is raw in salads. And the most popular nonsalad lettuce role is in sandwiches. Can we agree that the high point of human achievement in this popular category is the BLT? Of course, we can, which means that we share an affection for iceberg lettuce, that much-scorned-as-plebeian, crunchy leaf so indispensable as a companion to tomatoes, bacon, mayonnaise, and toasted white bread.

Muscardinus avellanarius, a bushy-tailed, mouselike rodent fond of hazelnuts, as its name implies, the dormouse sleeps most of the day in a cocoonlike nest, just like the narcoleptic Dormouse in *Alice's Adventures in Wonderland.* Petronius calls the little fellow *glis.*

†*Lactuca* is the classical Latin word for lettuce, used by Pliny and Virgil. It derives from *lac,* milk, because the midribs of its leaves yield a milky latex.

cuốn diếp
vietnamese lettuce roll

Do you think it is pretentious that I have insisted on including the polytonic* accents on the Vietnamese name of this lettuce roll and its fermented fish sauce? I definitely have no idea what they portend as to pronunciation. My spoken Vietnamese is limited, to say the least. But I am proud of being able to get these exotic marks to display on my computer screen.[†]

The culinary interest of this recipe is also polytonic, so to speak. First, and foremost for our current purposes, is the use of lettuce instead of the emblematically Vietnamese rice-pancake "spring roll" skin called *bánh tráng*. These skins are much crisper than their Chinese counterparts and, after they have been softened with egg yolk, are the canonical wrappers for the omnipresent spring rolls called *chả giò*.

Second, these equally ubiquitous lettuce rolls are wrapped in raw lettuce, a feature of some Chinese dishes, but what is germane here is that the raw lettuce provides the crunch all by itself that bánh tráng do for chá giò after being soaked in egg and then fried. Whatever lettuce they use in Danang, the locally available American alternative would seem to be iceberg.

Third, the ineluctable Vietnamese fish sauce *nước mắm* is, however challenging it may be to the palates of round-eyed first-timers, a living ringer for the oldest recorded sauce in the Western tradition: *garum*. This barrel-fermented, anchovy-based condiment was a fundamental feature of cooking in ancient Rome.

1 iceberg lettuce

4 ounces (¼ package) medium rice sticks (*bún*) or 1 packet of thin Japanese wheat noodles (*somen*), boiled for 2 or 3 minutes, drained, and cooled under cold water

½ pound medium shrimp, boiled, shelled, and halved lengthwise

½ pound pork belly or other boneless pork, boiled for 20 minutes and sliced into noodle-thin 2-inch by 1-inch strips

1 handful mint leaves

1 handful coriander leaves (cilantro), roughly chopped

*More than one diacritical mark per letter. Ancient Greek is a polytonic language.

[†]In Microsoft Word's standard toolbar, click on Insert, then in the menu that appears, click on Symbol. Find the character you want, click on it, and then click the box labeled SUBMIT. This will cause the desired character to appear where you left the cursor in the file you were creating. Of course, if you have a Vietnamese font installed on your computer, this dodge is unnecessary.

1 bunch scallion greens, blanched for 30 seconds
One recipe Nước Chấm Sauce (recipe follows)

1. Cut the lettuce leaves in half along the central vein. Rinse and dry.

2. Lay out the lettuce leaves on a clean counter. At the root end of each piece, place 2 tablespoons noodles, a shrimp half, a pork slice, 3 mint leaves, and a pinch of chopped coriander leaves. Roll up tightly and tie in the middle with a scallion green. If any lettuce leaves are left over, use them in a green salad at another time.

3. Trim the ends of the rolls and place on a serving platter. Pass the Nước Chấm Sauce.

Serves 6

nước chấm sauce

2 garlic cloves, peeled

4 dried red chile peppers, trimmed and seeded

4 teaspoons sugar

Juice of ½ lime

¼ cup nước mắm (Vietnamese bottled fish sauce)

1. Pound the garlic, chiles, and sugar to a paste in a mortar. Stir in the lime juice.

2. Cut away the lime pulp, chop roughly, and add to the sauce along with the fish sauce and 4 tablespoons water. Stir together and serve.

molokheya

Molokheya is a leafy green plant, like spinach in appearance but not in taste. Its Latin name is *Corchorus olitorius*. Vernacular names include Jew's mallow, jute mallow, and nalta jute. As the last two names suggest, *C. olitorius* is a source of the crude fiber known either as jute or burlap and was once made into bags called gunny.

In North Africa, especially Egypt, the leaves, fresh, dried, or frozen, are eaten, usually in a soup, which they thicken and color green.

egyptian molokheya soup

This is the national soup of Egypt. The elite version is prepared with rabbit, but chicken is common and acceptable. Khalid M. Baheyeldin, a computer engineer from Alexandria now based in Canada, maintains a Web site (Baheyeldin.com) containing, among much else, lore about molokheya. It transpires that a millennium ago the "mad Fatimid caliph al-Hakim bi Amrillah" forbade his subjects to eat molokheya. Why? Because "Mu'awya ibn Abi Sufyan, the arch-enemy of the Shia used to like it!" People caught with molokheya were flogged. A later ruler, al-Zahir, relaxed the prohibition.

Mr. Baheyeldin goes on to quote several translations of Tale 43 of the *Arabian Nights* ("The Man of Yemen and His Six Slave Girls"), in which one concubine derides another by comparing her to an inferior kind of molokheya grown in a poor quarter of Cairo, Bab al-Luq. The Burton translation is rich and strange:

> *My form is all grace and my shape is built on heavy base; Kings desire my colour which all adore, rich and poor. I am pleasant, active, handsome, elegant, soft of skin and prized for price: eke I am perfect in seemlibead [sic] and breeding and eloquence; my aspect is comely and my tongue witty; my temper is bright and my play a pretty sight. Thou art like unto a mallow growing about the Lúk gate; in hue sallow and streaked-yellow and made all of sulphur. Aroynt thee, O copper-worth of jaundiced sorrel, O rust of brass-pot, O face of owl in gloom, and fruit of the Hell-tree Zakkúm. . . .*

1½ pounds dried or frozen molokheya leaves, picked clean of twigs and stones if necessary*

9 cups chicken stock

3 tablespoons olive oil

1 head garlic, peeled and finely chopped

2 tablespoons finely chopped fresh coriander leaves

1 tablespoon ground coriander

Salt

1 teaspoon black pepper

1. If you use fresh molokheya leaves, chop them as fine as possible, or if you are feeling in an energetic mood, grab a handful, press it into a tight ball, and shred the leaves into very fine slivers. If you use frozen leaves, put them, undefrosted, in a 3-quart saucepan.

2. Pour the chicken stock over the leaves. Bring to a boil, reduce the heat, and simmer for 20 minutes.

3. Meanwhile, heat the olive oil in a small skillet and brown the garlic in it. Add to the soup after the molokheya has disintegrated.

4. When the soup is finished, add the chopped coriander leaves, ground coriander, and salt and pepper to taste.

Serves 6 to 8

*Thirty years ago, following a recipe of Claudia Roden, I used dried molokheya leaves, purchased at Sahadi's market in the Arab district of Atlantic Avenue in South Brooklyn. All was going well until I reached the stage where Ms. Roden called for pureeing the soup in a blender. I threw the switch; there was a loud, explosive noise; and the soup poured out of a small hole in the base of the blender jar. I had not managed to remove a small stone lurking among the leaves. My conclusion was that it was the wrong historical moment for one Jew to be telling another how to make the national soup of Egypt. You will note that the recipe above does not call for a blender.

mushrooms

Mushroom is a humble-sounding name for one of the major divisions of life.* Scientists call it the fungi kingdom. Ordinary folk divide this kingdom into the edible (mushrooms) and the inedible (toadstools), because they are either toxic, lethal, or unpleasant to eat. My grandfather believed that you could tell the difference between the two by boiling them and then putting a silver spoon in the cooking liquid. Toadstools turned the spoon black.[†]

In fact, mycophiles must master a far more sophisticated system of identification requiring spore prints, knowledge of the arcana of how gills attach to stipes, and facility with a low-powered magnifying glass as well as the diagnostic powers of Meltzer's solution. But even the untutored stand a fairly good chance of living their normal span because relatively few species are lethal or even seriously toxic. This should not be taken as encouragement to stuff any old fungus in your mouth. Some very common mushrooms will destroy your liver lickety-split.

Another word of warning: If you do learn to identify safe edible mushrooms in the field, don't brag about it. Once your skill becomes known, you lose the chance to eliminate a hated spouse or parent by "innocently" serving them toothsome caps of *Amanita virosa* in cream on toast.

That said, the increasing availability of the choicest varieties of wild mushrooms in groceries eliminates the need for foraging on your own.

Virtually all mushrooms can be sautéed in butter or oil. They are full of water; that's why they "mushroom" on lawns and in forests overnight after rainstorms. The first few minutes of cooking force them to give up their water. Eventually it boils away and the remaining butter or oil rises in temperature above 212 degrees, signaling the commencement of this stage with a sizzling noise. Toss the mushrooms, whisk in some heavy cream, and serve. The delicious fats will have replaced the water in the mushrooms' cells, preserving their shape and improving their flavor and mouthfeel.

The six recipes that follow go beyond this universal method with an ingenuity that has made them classics.

---

*Unlike "toadstool," which is purely fanciful, "mushroom" only sounds twee. The OED traces it to a variety of Anglo-Norman words whose vestige in modern French is *mousseron*, a vernacular term for the mushroom *Clitopilus prunulus*. This kind of taxonomic accuracy is a thing of the present. *Mousseron* would have applied not so long ago to a nonspecific smear of fungi, and, despite the dubiety of lexicographers, its origin looks blindingly clear to an outsider. It must come from *mousse*-moss, another spontaneous growth on woody surfaces.

†Grandpa survived his magical thinking only to succumb to death-by-opera. After a lifetime of listening to the Saturday radio broadcasts of the Metropolitan Opera, without ever having seen an opera onstage, until in 1949 he acquired a television in time for the opening-night telecast of *Der Rosenkavalier* on November 21, with Fritz Reiner conducting Eleanor Steber, Risë Stevens, Giuseppe di Stefano, and Erna Berger. He expired from bliss during the first intermission.

cèpes à la bordelaise
porcini with shallots

These large, fleshy bolete mushrooms are delicacies the world over. If you turn over one of the caps you will not see gills, but rather a spongy, often yellow surface full of tiny tubules. Italians dry them so that any cook can rehydrate and serve them all year long. In Italy, you sometimes see fresh porcini as large as the plate you are eating them on. They do not taste better than less Brogdingnagian ones you can cook in this pure, chaste style. *À la bordelaise* literally means in the style of Bordeaux. However, if you try to connect this recipe with the great city of southwest France, you will be barking up the wrong stipe. Like almost all of the epithets which French haute cuisine attached to its myriad dishes, bordelaise has nothing to do with the actual regional cuisine of Bordeaux.

It is a code that tells the clued-in chef or diner what she is about to make or eat. Often there is a vague link to ingredients a Parisian might associate with the place (Spain/tomatoes) that inspired some cook who had never been there to name what he'd cooked (sauce espagnole, a classic brown sauce with tomatoes added toward the end of its lengthy preparation).

À la bordelaise is, in fact, an unhelpfully complex example of this process of factitious encoding. *Larousse Gastronomique*, in its authoritative edition of 1938, specifies no less than four very distinct meanings for the term (apart from various desserts with Bordeaux in their names). The most logical is for a sauce containing wine, the most famous product of Bordeaux, and beef marrow. Two do not seem especially bordelais at all—dishes containing mirepoix* and those garnished with artichokes and potatoes. The fourth refers to dishes containing boletes, which do in fact grow abundantly in southwest France.

1¾ pounds fresh porcini

1 cup non-olive oil

Salt

Pepper

2 tablespoons butter

6 shallots, peeled and finely chopped

½ lemon

2 teaspoons finely chopped parsley

1. Cut away the bottom of the stipe and discard. Then cut off the stipes from the caps of the mushrooms. Cut a ½-inch piece from the cap end of each stipe, chop finely, and reserve. Unless you want to keep the rest of the stipes for a soup, discard them.

2. Cut the caps into ½-inch slices.

3. Heat ¾ cup of the oil in a skillet until it begins to smoke. Add the mushroom slices and brown them for 2 minutes on each side (turn with a tongs). When the slices are nicely browned, reduce the heat to low and continue to cook for 5 minutes. Raise the heat to high and cook for another 2 minutes, turning once.

4. Put a cover over the skillet. Raise the skillet with one hand and hold the cover on with the other. Pour off all the oil into a saucepan. Uncover the skillet and set it down on a cold burner. Sprinkle the mushrooms with salt and pepper. Return the skillet to the heat. Sauté over high heat briefly to distribute the salt and pepper. Transfer the mushroom slices to a serving dish and keep warm in a low oven.

5. Heat the reserved oil with the butter. When the mixture begins to smoke, toss in the chopped stipes and the shallots. Cook for 1 minute, then pour all the contents of the saucepan over the mushroom slices. Squeeze the lemon over them. Sprinkle on the parsley and serve immediately.

Serves 6

*Mirepoix is an appareil, a chef's concoction prepared in advance (see page 58 and the recipe for Dux-elles, page 155), in this case a mixture of diced carrots, onions, and raw ham sautéed together with a bouquet garni (sprigs of parsley and thyme tied together in a bundle with a bay leaf). The name Mire-poix is a curious bedfellow with Bordeaux, since Mirepoix is a provincial town in the department of the Ariège (a river), far to the southeast.

champignons à la lucien tendret
mushrooms in the manner of lucien tendret

Lucien Tendret was the nephew of the great food writer and aphorist Brillat-Savarin. Tendret, himself a food writer, never left the family hometown of Belley, the provincial capital of a subregion, the Bugey, east of Lyon near Bourg-en-Bresse. In short, Tendret was a late-nineteenth-century country squire and lawyer whose sole distinction was his uncle. Not one to shrink from playing his only trump, Tendret published a pompous memoir of the cuisine of the Bugey in 1892 called *La table au pays de Brillat-Savarin*. It contains recipes for some grandiose dishes described in a fatuous and inflated prose. It is also a meticulous and winsome memoir of bourgeois ataraxy in those last few decades before the storm of modern life shattered his world. He was a minor writer, definitely.

But miniature masterpieces have their place. Tendret's elegant turn on the basic recipe for sautéed mushrooms is comfort food for the already comfortable. If anybody cooks it in Belley today, she works off the calories at the municipal tennis courts on the avenue Lucien Tendret.

1 pound mushrooms, gently rinsed and trimmed
1 tablespoon butter
1 tablespoon flour
5 tablespoons beef stock
1 cup heavy cream
Salt
White pepper
1 egg yolk

1. Slice the mushrooms lengthwise. You should end up with about 5 cups.
2. Melt the butter in a large skillet. It should just coat the bottom of the pan. Add the mushroom slices and sauté over medium-high heat. They will quickly release a significant quantity of water. When this boils away, lower the heat to low-medium. Sprinkle the flour over the mushrooms and stir well. Continue stirring while the flour browns, about 10 minutes.
3. Stir in 1 tablespoon of the stock. Then stir in the cream. Simmer for 20 minutes. This will reduce and thicken the cream to a rich sauce. Season with salt and white pepper.
4. While the cream reduces, whisk the egg yolk into the remaining ¼ cup stock.

5. Remove the mushroom-cream mixture from the heat after the cream has reduced. Whisk the egg yolk–stock mixture into it. This will finish the sauce, giving it a richer, darker color, and the action of the hot cream on the egg yolk will thicken it further.

Serves 4

duxelles

In a simple time before chemists had concocted synthetic flavorings, chefs made their own natural ones from real ingredients. Duxelles, a classic such chef-made food additive, or appareil, is an intense, dehydrated source of mushroom essence. It was most probably invented by Henri IV's great chef, François-Pierre de la Varenne, author of *Le Cuisinier François* (1651), when he was working for the Marquis d'Uxelles.

1 pound mushrooms, trimmed, rinsed, and finely chopped

6 tablespoons butter

4 medium onions, about ¾ pound, peeled and finely chopped

10 shallots, peeled and finely chopped

½ teaspoon salt

½ teaspoon pepper

¼ teaspoon ground nutmeg

1. Wrap the mushrooms in a dishtowel. Twist from both ends over a mixing bowl to extract as much liquid as possible. Scrape the mushrooms from the towel into a bowl and set aside. Reserve the extracted mushroom liquid for a soup.

2. Melt the butter in a large skillet over medium-high heat. When the foam subsides, stir in the chopped onions and shallots. Sauté until they turn straw-gold in color, stirring constantly with a wooden spoon.

3. Add the mushrooms, along with the seasonings. Stir over high heat, while the mushroom particles cook and then give up their liquid. Continue cooking until the liquid boils away. The sign of this is a sudden sizzling sound, the sound of butter rising in temperature in the absence of water. Remove from the heat and scrape into a storage container. Duxelles will keep in the refrigerator for several weeks. For longer storage, freeze.

Makes 2½ to 3 cups

huitlacoche soup

Long before the disruptive arrival of Cortés in 1519, Aztecs and other indigenous peoples dealt creatively with the limited larder of pre–Hispanic Mexico. The insects and the pond scum that rounded out their diet are curiosities now, but *huitlacoche,** aka corn smut, is a treasured delicacy throughout the world.

Well, not everywhere. Although this black fungus colonizes ears of corn as far away from the Valley of Mexico as Iowa, American corn farmers tend to see it as a blight. Like those Great Lakes fishermen who fight to kill lampreys instead of catching and eating them, these stewards of our most characteristic grain shun huitlacoche when they could be selling it to gourmets at farmstands.

Mexicans armed with European ideas now serve huitlacoche in crepes and other *raffiné* dishes. This soup puts the smut back together with the corn. The taste is mild and smoky. The chopped chiles liven things up, but the real Mexican stamp is the herb epazote, with a taste so distinctive that we recognized it in the Philippines. Epazote grows all over North America as a weed in vacant lots. Mexican grocers invariably sell it.

2 tablespoons lard
1 small onion, peeled and chopped fine
4 garlic cloves, peeled and chopped fine
2 cups huitlacoche, roughly chopped
1 cup corn kernels
1 epazote sprig
4 cups chicken stock
Salt
Pepper
4 serrano chiles, chopped

1. Melt the lard in an 8-cup saucepan. Then sauté the onion and garlic until the onion has turned translucent. Stir in the huitlacoche, the corn kernels, and the epazote. Cover and sweat for 10 minutes, stirring frequently. Add a bit of chicken stock if the corn starts sticking.

2. Add the rest of the stock and season with salt and pepper. Serve with serrano chiles on the side.

Serves 4 to 6

*This Nahuatl word is sometimes spelled cuitlacoche, indicating a faint *k* sound at the beginning. Even native Nahuatl speakers will not mind if you miss this nuance and just say: Wheat-la-ko-che (as in Guevara).

morels in cream

Pocked, rounded coneheads peek out of the duff and silently offer themselves to the sharp-eyed forager. These are morels, *Morchella* spp., premier mushrooms for the table. Unlike most mushrooms we eat (basidiomycetes, those club mushrooms with solid heads) morels are ascomycetes, sack mushrooms with hollow heads. They are foolproof to identify in the field. I once found four pounds in an afternoon, a very fine afternoon. Because they are hollow, you can stuff morels. Because of the odd and unforgettable apearance of their heads, you can use a couple at a time to garnish chops or a steak. But I love them so much, I want to make them the center of the story. So here is the most prized of all mushrooms cooked in the most fundamental way possible.

1 pound morels
6 tablespoons butter
½ cup heavy cream
Salt
4 thin slices white bread

1. Slice the morels in half lengthwise. Rinse out any sand or other matter inside the cavity.

2. Melt 3 tablespoons of the butter in a skillet just large enough to hold the morels. When the foam subsides, add the morels. Lower the heat to medium and stir until the mushrooms give up their water. The sign of this is steam rising from the pan. Continue simmering until the water evaporates and the mushrooms begin to simmer in the butter. Stir-fry until the mushrooms are completely covered with butter.

3. Pour in the cream. Bring to a boil, remove from the heat, and add salt to taste.

4. Melt the remaining 3 tablespoons butter in a clean skillet. Cut the bread slices in half diagonally (into triangles). Fry them in the butter until they are golden brown. Drain on paper toweling.

5. Place the fried bread triangles on four plates, two to a plate. Pour a quarter of the mushrooms over each plate. Serve.

Serves 4

mushrooms à la grecque
greek-style mushrooms

There is a reason why these blanched, boldly seasoned mushrooms are ubiquitous as first courses in busy, unpretentious restaurants from L'Île sur la Sorgue to Konya. They are incredibly easy to make. And they have a wonderful texture and flavor because they exploit the mushrooms' ability to pick up flavors. Here they are napped in a reduction of their cooking liquid. I can also recommend marinating mushrooms in the same seasonings and olive oil. They are raw but tempered by the oil they have absorbed.

 2 teaspoons salt
½ cup vinegar
10 peppercorns
8 coriander seeds
8 fennel seeds
1½ pounds mushrooms, wiped clean and halved lengthwise

1. Bring 2¾ cups of water to a boil. Add all the ingredients except the mushrooms. Simmer for 5 minutes, covered.

2. Add the mushrooms and simmer for 10 minutes, covered. Remove the mushrooms to a serving bowl with a slotted spoon.

3. Reduce the cooking liquid at a full rolling boil, uncovered, until it turns viscous. Pour over the mushrooms (through a strainer if you don't like the homey look of peppercorns and coriander seeds). Let cool. Serve at room temperature.

Serves 6

napa cabbage

kimchi

There are as many kimchis as there are Koreans.* In the Korean diaspora as well as in Korea itself, the basic pickled cabbage, *tongkimchi*, which is the national condiment, the national dish, and the national folk panacea, starts out as Napa cabbage (aka nappa or celery cabbage or Chinese cabbage or in Korean, *baechu* [*Brassica rapa* var. *pekinensis*]), the big white-and-green, watery, crunchy cabbage now common in our markets.

The fermentation is a basic lactic-acid fermentation in a crock in brine. The cabbage leaves are first softened in the brine, then coated with the other ingredients, including pickled fish, tied up in packages, and left to ferment in the crock. Koreans have traditionally made their own kimchi, usually in the fall, the so-called *kimjang*, or kimchi-making season. Special markets open to sell standard ingredients. Corporations give kimjang bonuses to help workers out with the expense of making the huge quantities of kimchi that supply them with vegetable nutrition throughout the winter. By burying sealed crocks, they can keep a batch for several weeks in cold weather.

Kimchi is also an ingredient in many "made" dishes, especially soups and one-pot casseroles.

Koreans began pickling vegetables as far back as the twelfth century, but chiles did not become widely available until the eighteenth century, while Chinese cabbage was not introduced until the nineteenth. The name "kimchi" may have begun as *shimchae* (salted vegetables) and then evolved to *dimchae*, then to *kimchae*, and finally to modern kimchi. Many claims for the health-giving qualities of kimchi are made by proud, kimchi-loving Koreans. And Koreans act on these claims by eating even more kimchi than normal when disease threatens.

During the SARS scare, kimchi consumption went up. And in the spring of 2005, the same thing happened after scientists fed kimchi to thirteen chickens infected with avian flu. Eleven recovered.

* 48.5 million in South Korea alone. A short list of kimchi varieties includes:
- Whole Cabbage Kimchi (*Tongbaechu gimchi*)
- Wrapped-up Kimchi (*Possam gimchi*)
- White Cabbage Kimchi (*Paekkimchi*)—it is not hot, so you may enjoy it!
- Radish Kimchi (*Yolmugimchi*)
- Water Kimchi with Fresh Ginseng (*Susamnabakkimchi*)—for your health!
- Whole Radish Kimchi (*Altarigimchi*)
- Radish Water Kimchi (*Tongchimi*)
- Stuffed Cucumber Kimchi (*Oisobagi*)
- Hot Radish Kimchi (*Kkakttugi*)

½ cup pickled corvina, a Pacific fish, available in Korean markets, cut into julienne strips

5 heads Napa cabbage

3½ cups kosher salt

2 white Korean radishes, trimmed and cut into julienne strips

1 cup cayenne, moistened to make a paste

White parts of 4 scallions, trimmed and cut into 2-inch sections

½ bundle "green-thread" onions or Chinese scallions, cut into 2-inch lengths

½ bundle Indian mustard leaves

Korean watercress, cut into 2-inch lengths

¾ pound sponge seaweed, cut into 2-inch pieces

2 heads garlic, peeled and pureed in a garlic press

Two 3-inch pieces ginger, peeled and finely chopped

1 cup pickled baby shrimp, chopped

¾ pound shucked oysters, rinsed in lightly salted water

5 dried red chiles, seeded and cut into very thin "threads"

¼ cup sugar

1. Cut the pickled corvina into thin strips and reserve. Boil the juice it was packed in with its bones and a little water for 10 minutes. Strain and reserve the liquid. Discard the bones.

2. Pull off the outer leaves of the cabbages and reserve. Cut the cabbages in half lengthwise, starting from the bottom and stopping one-third of the way in. Complete the splitting of the cabbages with your hands. This does less damage to the inner leaves than a knife would.

3. In a nonaluminum pot or crock large enough to hold all the cabbages, make a brine with 3 cups of the salt and 1 gallon (16 cups) of cold water. Stir until the salt has dissolved. Then immerse the cabbage halves and the reserved outer leaves. Let them soak for 4 hours, or until softened. Rinse thoroughly and drain.

4. In a large mixing bowl, stir together the radish strips and the red pepper paste. Let stand for a half hour. Then mix in all the remaining ingredients.

5. Spread all the leaves with the mixture from step 4. Wrap each filled cabbage half tightly with one of the reserved outer leaves. Set the wrapped cabbages back in the crock. Cover them with the remaining outer leaves. Press down on them lightly. Let the kimchi stand at room temperature for 24 hours in summer, or for 2 days the rest of the year. Then refrigerate. It will keep for a week or possibly more.

Makes 10 pickled cabbage halves

okra

Even if you find the mucilaginous material (slime to its enemies) exuded by the ridged pods of okra repulsive, you cannot help but be seduced by the mazy thicket of its nomenclature and its botanical relatives. The traditional and only partially obsolete Linnaean name is *Abelmoschus esculentus*, literally the edible "father of musk." This Saddamian formulation probably came about because the hibiscus-like flowers of the okra plant smelled to some early arabophone botanizer like the true musk he had met at table. The resemblance to hibiscus blooms is not superficial but fundamental. Indeed, the revised standard name for okra is now *Hibiscus esculentus*, which puts it in the same genus as all those gloriously blooming plants arranged in such floral splendor in the Fairchild Tropical Botanic Garden in Coral Gables, Fla.—until feral iguanas ate them.

More to the point, both okra and hibiscus belong to the huge mallow family, Malvaceae, which includes such other familiar plants as the durian, the magnolia, and the molokheya, or Jew's mallow of North Africa (see page 146). Hibiscus petals (technically not from the flowers but the calyx) are the sole ingredient of a tea popular in the Caribbean and Mexico as *rosa de Jamaica*. That particular hibiscus goes by the vernacular name "roselle." For the complete (and completely fascinating) lowdown on it and its history, log on to http://www.hort.purdue.edu/newcrop/ Indices/index_ab.html.

fried bhindi

Bhindi is Hindi for okra. I apologize for the rhyme but it is impossible to avoid unless you use one of the other, mostly African names for the plant that have followed its peregrinations around the globe. The main alternative is gumbo, the U.S. Creole reflex of the Angolan Bantu *ki ngombo*, which led to *quingombo* in Portuguese or *quimbombó* in Cuban Spanish,* or *gombo* in French.[†]

Fried okra is an idea that belongs to the world. In India, the spice mixture naturalizes the recipe, just as "Southern-fried" okra belongs to the former centers of slave population in the Americas. The best fried okra I have tasted was at a large barbecue restaurant in Raleigh, N.C., where most patrons were black. It came out of the kitchen crisp outside, just barely cooked through inside, and not at all slimy.

¼ cup sesame seeds

2 tablespoons white poppy seeds

3 to 4 dried chiles, trimmed and seeded

6 tablespoons any vegetable oil except olive oil

1 teaspoon black mustard seeds

½ teaspoon fenugreek seeds

4 garlic cloves, peeled and finely chopped

1 pound okra, topped, tailed, and cut in ½-inch rounds

Salt

Fresh green chiles, chopped

1. Heat a kadhai or a heavy iron skillet over medium heat and dry-roast the sesame and poppy seeds until brown. Put the seeds along with the dried red chiles in a clean electric coffee grinder and pulverize. Reserve on a plate.

2. Heat the oil in the kadhai or skillet over medium heat and add the mustard seeds. As the seeds pop add the fenugreek, followed by the garlic. Brown the garlic and then add the okra and salt to taste. Stir and mix thoroughly. Lower the flame, cover, and cook for about 10 minutes, stirring occasionally.

3. Stir in the reserved ground sesame and poppy seeds and mix well. Remove from the flame and serve with chopped green chiles passed separately.

Serves 4

*Also the name of a dance band specializing in *son*, a type of Afro-Cuban music.

[†]There are many other vernacular names, of which *bamia* in Arabic is the widest spread.

okra and tomatoes

Whoever combined tomatoes and okra first was a fusion chef *avant la lettre*. Okra, a gift from Africa to the rest of the world, came westward across the Atlantic as an unintended consequence of the slave trade—and met the tomato on its native ground. It must actually have occurred to cook after cook that the acidity of the tomato would be a nice match for the mildly astringent and otherwise unassertive okra. Today, it is a classic combination, toned up with onions. The tomato disguises the sliminess of the okra.

3 tablespoons corn oil

2 garlic cloves, peeled and finely chopped

2 large onions, peeled and chopped

2 pounds okra, topped and tailed

1½ pounds canned Italian tomatoes

1 dried red chile, seeded and crumbled, or cayenne

Salt and pepper

1. Heat the oil in a cast-iron skillet until a sliver of garlic tossed in it sizzles. Lower the heat to medium. Add the garlic and cook until it starts to brown. Then add the onions and cook until the pieces are translucent.

2. Add the okra, the tomatoes and any liquid from the can, the crumbled chile or cayenne to taste, the salt and the pepper.

3. Stir the mixture together gently, leaving the tomatoes intact. When the okra has softened just enough to chew easily, remove the skillet from the heat and serve. Or cool and refrigerate until you are ready to serve it. It will reheat nicely, but be careful not to overcook the okra in the process.

Serves 6 as a side dish with fried chicken

seafood gumbo

"Jambalaya, a crawfish pie and a filé gumbo"

—Hank Williams, Sr.

The song was a big hit in 1952, especially in the decountrified cover by Jo Stafford with the Norman Luboff Choir, hitting number 3 on the *Billboard* pop chart. Only a few grinches criticized Williams's fractured Cajun French. But did anyone notice the biggest barbarism in his lyrics, that gastronomic hippogriff "filé gumbo"?

A gumbo is a soup of Cajun Louisiana thickened *either* by okra (gumbo) *or* by filé, the powdered leaves of *Sassafras albidum*, the common sassafras tree, which is (or actually was) the main active ingredient of root beer. But no well-trained Cajun cook puts okra and filé in the same gumbo. The tradition is firm as iron, but it rests on the practical fact that either one of these down-home thickeners was enough to make a spoon stand up in a gumbo. Two was as silly as wearing a belt and suspenders.

In 1952, this would have been a possible mistake. Today, it would be a crime. I was still able to buy filé legally in a New Orleans grocery store in 1972, commercially bottled and labeled.* Subsequent scientific analysis showed that sassafras contained dangerous amounts of safrole, a carcinogenic oil; in chemist's lingo it is an aphenolic ether, which is also a precursor to a form of amphetamine and can cause not only cancer but menstrual irregularity, low sperm count, and degradation of the nervous system (but not all three in the same person). Safrole is also used to manufacture the drug Ecstasy. Since sassafras trees still are at large and produce leaves, anyone with access to one can easily make her own filé but with greater efficiency than the Choctaws, the original filé users, because a food processor is a great assist in turning dried leaves to powder. My advice is, stick to okra.

½ cup any vegetable oil except olive oil

4 pounds chicken wings

2 garlic cloves, peeled and finely chopped

⅔ cup flour

¾ pound ham, diced

¾ pound onions, peeled and chopped

1 large green pepper, chopped

4 scallions, trimmed and chopped (white and green parts)

1½ pounds kielbasa or other smoked sausage, cut into ½-inch rounds

2½ pounds okra, topped and tailed

1 tablespoon salt

2 teaspoons black pepper

Cayenne to taste

6 thyme sprigs or 1 teaspoon dried thyme

2 bay leaves, crumbled

2 cups long-grain rice, boiled in a large quantity of lightly salted water until al dente, drained

1. Heat the oil in a large saucepan or Dutch oven until it begins to smoke and brown the chicken wings in it, a few at a time. Drain on paper toweling and reserve.

2. Remove the oil from the heat for a few minutes so that it cools. Place over low-medium heat and add the garlic. When it begins to brown, remove with a slotted spoon and reserve. Whisk in the flour and keep whisking until the oil and flour amalgamate and eventually turn into a brown mass the color of peanut butter or perhaps a touch darker.

3. Stir in the onions, green pepper, scallions, kielbasa, and the okra. Stir together, still over low-medium heat, until the onions turn transparent. Then add 9 cups of water, the reserved chicken and garlic, and all the seasonings. Bring to a boil, then reduce the heat, and simmer for 20 minutes, or until the wings are tender but not falling apart.

4. Add the rice to the gumbo. Make sure it is heated through. Then serve.

Serves 8 to 10

*This was a big help to me, because on that same trip I carried my souvenir of Louisiana in my luggage to two other centers of Creole cookery, Martinique and Guadeloupe. U.S. customs discovered the brownish-green powder as I reentered the country, but after some hesitation and much sniffing, the agent let me through with my filé.

onions

Everybody knows his onions, although some aspects of their biological and culinary nature are probably worth laying out here. For example, the Latin species name includes the genus *Allium*, the word for garlic, whose reflex in French is *ail* (pronounced "I"), and whose plural can be either the orthographically offputting but more usual *aulx* (pronounced "O") or the botanical *ails* (pronounced "I"). *Cepa*, condensed from the more common *caepa*, just meant onion, or whatever passed for an onion in ancient Italy. It is the source of many modern European words for onion: Spanish *cebolla*, Italian *cipolla*, Portuguese *cipola*, even German *Zwiebel*. Our "onion," an obvious descendant of French *oignon*, is really a close if historically distant relative of classical Latin *unio*, a single onion.

Columella, the agricultural authority (*fl*. A.D. 50) wrote: *"caepam, quam vocant unionem rustici."* When peasants talk about onions, they say *unio*. So it would seem that French and English inherited the rustic term, while the rest of Romance Europe held on to the polite word.

Our proper or "bulb" onions come in many colors and sizes, all of them produced at some distant time by cultivation. Records go back five thousand years, but there is a hypothesis that cultivated onions were coaxed out of wild types at some even more remote date in what is now Afghanistan or Iran.

Whatever. As those chainsmoking yuppies who are mystified by terms like "Churchill" and "icebox" might say. Fortunately, their cult of sentimental or paranoid vegetarianism does not prevent them from trying their mettle against onions. Inevitably, like the rest of us in the varicose population, some of them cry, in reaction to the volatile chemicals released from sulfurous elements in onions by enzymatic action, after the overlapping leaf clusters that form onion bulbs have been traumatized by a knife.

fegato* alla veneziana
sautéed liver and onions, as in venice

Done in a flash, this astute matchup muffles the bitterness of liver with the sweetness of the onions. So why do I bother taking expensive calf's liver, which is much gentler on the taste buds than plain old beef liver, and then gentle it in a milk bath? You can't be too careful.

2 pounds calf's liver, sliced very thin, about ¼ inch thick
2 cups milk
¼ cup olive oil
1¼ pounds yellow onions, peeled and thinly sliced
Salt and pepper

1. Trim away the membranes from the liver and cut it into strips about 1½ inches wide. Soak in the milk at room temperature for an hour.

2. Heat the olive oil in a large pot over medium heat. Add the onion slices and cook, stirring occasionally, until they turn brown. Remove the slices with a slotted spoon to a bowl and reserve until you are ready to cook the liver and serve it. Leave the residual oil in the skillet.

*If you happen to order this in Venice, or elsewhere in Italy, or even in an Italian restaurant, try to stifle your completely reasonable impulse to put the stress on the second syllable (officially the penult, second from the rear) of *fegato*. Unfortunately, for you and other logical folk not totally fluent in Italian, *fegato* is accented on its first syllable (the antepenult, third back); it looks like all those other Italian words ending in *-ato* and even in *-gato* that *are* accented on the penult. But they are past participles of first conjugation verbs whose infinitives end in *-are*, including words common in English or on menus: *legato, affogato*.

Fegato, on the other hand is a noun, which, like its French cognate *foie*, comes not from the Latin noun for liver, *jecur*, but from the noun *ficatum*, a liver from a goose fed on figs, an ur-foie gras.

We know from a graffito at Pompeii that this delicacy started out as *jecur ficatum*, a figged liver, but then got curtailed to plain *ficatum*. So why didn't this participle get accented on the penult like all the others I've mentioned?

Pliny the Younger wrote an eyewitness account of the eruption of the Mt. Vesuvius in the year 79. His father, Pliny the Elder, died in the conflagration, and the city of Pompeii was buried—and thereby preserved—in ash. Unfortunately, neither Pliny nor anyone else explained how the Pompeiian delicacy *ficatum* was pronounced. The poet Horace referred (in Satires 2.88) to the liver of a white goose fattened with lush figs (*pinguibus et ficis pastum iecur anseris albae*), but the lovely line doesn't include

3. Just before you intend to serve this dish, heat the oil until it smokes. Add the liver strips all at once and stir-fry them for a minute or two, until they lose their pink color. Add the reserved onions, the salt and the pepper, and stir together with the liver. Serve as soon as the onions have reheated.

Serves 6

our participle, only a form of the noun for fig (*ficus*). But the fig may well be the explanation for the *fegato* conundrum.

Italian took over the Latin *ficus* and converted it to *fico*. Along the way, fig acquired an obscene second meaning, the equivalent of cunt. Wily Italians then invented a new word almost exactly like *fico*, except for the last letter. *Fica* became the official dirty word for vulva (in classical Latin, the preferred spelling was *volva*, which basically meant a cover or wrapping, and, by extension, the uterus), as well as the name for an obscene gesture in which the thumb is placed between the index and middle finger and then thrust upward.

My friend Paul Levy, the Kentucky-born British food writer, once hosted a dinner in London for a group of foodies. He seated himself between me and a professor of anatomy at Cambridge. By dessert time, conversation lagged. I heard Levy try to enliven things by asking the anatomist what his area of special interest within anatomy was. The professor replied: "Why, Paul, I'm a vulvologist."

While I choked on a piece of cake, Levy, cool as a walrus, responded: "I see that both of us have chosen a subject everyone cares about. We've just gone further into it."

It is my guess that this pudic cleansing of *fico* had the secondary effect of making the liver difficult to mention in polite society. *Ficatum* no longer meant just figged liver (really the liver itself by this point in time); it now contained within it the new word *fica*. And since *ficatum* would still have been felt to be a participle, *ficatum* acquired an obscene sense rather like our "fucked." No pun or etymology intended. "Fuck" is an Anglo-Saxon word with the same ancestry as German *ficken*.

Once again, Italians solved the problem they had created for themselves. By distorting the spelling and the pronunciation of *ficatum*, they purified the liver of its aural taint. The *i* became *e*, and the accent got moved back a syllable, eliminating the possibility of a double entendre. (The *c* had already changed to *g* in popular speech.) *Figa* is still the earthier colloquial form of *fica*. And so FÉgato was born, making it possible for Milanese women of fashion to complain daintily about their liver trouble, *male di fegato*.

onion bhajia

Bhajia (singular *bhaji*) is Hindi for fried vegetables. In the mostly Bangladeshi restaurants where I eat bhajia, they tend to be deep-fried balls of sliced onion in chickpea flour (*besan*) batter. There is no better hot appetizer than these crisp, spryly spiced vehicles for partially tamed onion. The word "bhaji" also tells us something about our Indo-European heritage. It derives from the Sanskrit *bhrajj*, the ancestor also of our word "fry." In addition to inventing the swastika, those old Aryans could fry.

2 teaspoons ground cumin

3 tablespoons any vegetable oil except olive oil

1½ cups besan (chickpea flour)

4 fresh green serrano chiles, trimmed, seeded, and chopped

Salt

3 medium onions, peeled and sliced

Any vegetable oil except olive oil, for deep-frying

1. In a medium bowl, mix together the ground cumin, the vegetable oil, the besan, the chopped chiles, and salt to taste. Beat in approximately ½ cup of cold water, or enough to make a batter. Whisk for a few minutes and then let stand for 2 hours, covered, at room temperature.

2. Heat 3 or 4 inches of oil in a kadhai or wok until the oil begins to smoke.

3. Whisk the onions into the batter. With a large serving ladle, pick up as much as you can of the onion mixture and lower it carefully into the oil. Let fry until the bhajia turns golden brown. Remove with a slotted spoon and let drain on paper toweling. Continue with the rest of the bhajia mixture in this manner.

Serves 4

onion rings

Vidalia is a town in Georgia that used to have the monopoly on a variety of large, sweet onions. Word spread about these Vidalia onions. Some smartypantses figured out how to grow them in other parts, but they still call them Vidalia. Frankly, I am not going to caterwaul against this piracy. As long as the Vidalias not from Vidalia are just as good as the ones that are from Vidalia, I will be happy to make superb onion rings with them. This is the recipe worth attempting, if you are ever going to overcome your fear of frying.

4 large Vidalia onions, peeled and sliced

3 cups buttermilk

2½ cups flour

2 cups yellow cornmeal

1 tablespoon salt

2 teaspoons cayenne

Oil for deep-frying

1. Soak the onion slices in the buttermilk for a half hour. Meanwhile, mix together the flour, the cornmeal, the salt, and the cayenne in a bowl.

2. Line two baking sheets with wax paper.

3. With a tongs, dip an onion ring in the batter. Let any excess drip off and set it on the wax paper. Continue until all the onion slices have been battered. Set the baking sheets in the refrigerator to chill for an hour.

4. Heat 3 to 4 inches of oil in a kadhai or wok to a temperature of approximately 360 degrees—hot enough to make a bit of batter sizzle, but not smoking hot. With a tongs, put 3 onion rings in the oil and fry until golden brown. Set on paper towels. Continue frying small batches until all the rings have been fried. Serve immediately.

Serves 6

onion soup

Onion soup is Holy Writ. Just ask anyone old enough to have made the midnight pilgrimage to Les Halles, the old central market of Paris, to have a bowl of cheese-topped *soupe a l'oignon* under the giant iron and glass pavilions filled with produce being pushed around by burly fellows (*les forts des Halles*) who took time off from their work to mock tourists or to couple with the *putes* hanging out nearby on the boulevard de Sébastopol or operating out of the dingy *hôtels de passe* on the narrow rue Quincampoix. Long since torn down, the market has moved out to suburban Rungis, where no one has ever gone for fun, to be replaced by the Pompidou Center's forced postindustrial gaiety. Because of the cheese melted over it, the Halles-style onion soup is familiarly called a *gratinée*. I'm all for getting rid of that ropy yellow toupee, and I find myself opting for unbrowned onions and chicken stock instead of the brawny darkness of the classic. But I will not try to impose this personal taste on you (the recipe is classic but offers options that will lead to a lighter soup).

You might also want to think about making a complete Halles meal, a real blast from the past, starting out with what habitués called "*un demi, demi*," a half dozen snails and a glass of beer (in theory a half liter but normally much less).

3 tablespoons butter
1 pound onions, peeled and finely chopped
12 slices French bread, lightly toasted
2 quarts beef or chicken stock
Salt
Pepper
½ pound grated Gruyère cheese

1. Melt the butter in a medium skillet and when the foam subsides, add the chopped onions and sauté slowly until they become a confit, browned and converted almost to a jam (or, alternatively, stop cooking when they are soft but not browned).

2. Preheat the oven to 450 degrees.

3. In a medium soup pot whose bottom will hold 3 bread slices in a single layer, add the bread slices in four overlapping layers. Add the onions. Pour on the hot beef stock (or chicken stock if you are using unbrowned onions and serve as is, without continuing on with this recipe), season briskly with salt and pepper, and then cover with an even layer of the grated cheese. Place in the oven, uncovered, and cook until the cheese has melted and is lightly browned. Serve immediately.

Serves 4 to 6

sauce soubise

Sauce Soubise is named after a noble house. Its first famous member was Benjamin, de Rohan, Duc de Soubise (1583–1642), leader of the Protestant faction during the reign of Louis XIII. He or his even more illustrious descendant, Prince Charles (1715–1782), a general defeated by Frederick the Great at Rossbach, may have taken credit for this onion coulis that goes so well with almost any meat or fish, but which is best known as a constituent of veal Prince Orloff. He also hired the architect Pierre Alexis Delamair to build the Hôtel de Soubise in Paris (1704), which now shelters the French National Archives.

4 tablespoons butter

1 pound onions, peeled and chopped fine

⅔ cup raw long-grain rice

2⅔ cups whole milk

Salt

White pepper

Sugar

½ cup heavy cream

1. Preheat the oven to 300 degrees.
2. Melt 2 tablespoons of the butter in a heavy 6-cup casserole over medium heat. Add the onions, cover, reduce the heat, and cook slowly, without browning, for 15 minutes.
3. Add the rice, the milk, and pinches of the salt, the white pepper, and the sugar. Bring to a boil, cover the casserole, and put it in the oven. Cook for 45 minutes. The rice will have absorbed most of the liquid and turned into a gruel or congee.
4. Process the mixture and then force it through a fine strainer into a saucepan. Add the remaining 2 tablespoons butter and the heavy cream. Stir together over low heat. Serve as a puree alongside roast chicken, veal, turkey, or as a filling in omelets.

Makes 2¼ cups

Variation: Beat in 2 tablespoons of tomato puree, or more, until you have achieved a color and taste you like.

parsnips

Fine words butter no parsnips, yes, but this neglected umbellifer deserves as much praise as possible. *Pastinaca sativa* has a flavor midway between sweet and earthy. Eclipsed after the potato took hold in Europe and abundant refined sugar made parsnip's sweetening ability obsolete, the parsnip has hung on, because its fleshy, white carrotlike taproots are so delicious and easy to cook. Although you are unlikely to come upon parsnips on a foreign menu, here, just in case, is a parsnip lexicon: French *panais*; German *Pastinake* or *Hammelmöhre* (mutton carrot); Italian *pastinaca*; Portuguese and Spanish *chirivia*; Russian *pasternak*.* The English name implies a resemblance to turnip ("neep" being an old word and the current Scottish name for turnip).

Parsnips have furrowed stems that resemble celery. The leaves are pointy and dark-green but probably not worth eating, since they contain furanocoumarins that sometimes cause skin irritation. These toxic substances protect the plant from its biggest enemy, the parsnip webworm. Human beings can develop "celery picker's itch" or "bartender's itch" after contact with parsnip leaves (as well as the oil of lime peel).

*A German loan word like many other Russian nouns, for example *Kartoffel* = potato. Boris Pasternak (1890–1960), author of *Dr. Zhivago*, won the Nobel Prize in literature in 1958.

jane grigson's buttered parsnips

1½ pounds parsnips

Salt

6 tablespoons butter

Pepper

2 tablespoons chopped parsley

1. Peel and trim the parsnips. Quarter them lengthwise. Cut out the centers if they are woody. Then slice the quarters into ¼-inch strips.

2. Bring 2 quarts of lightly salted water to a full boil. Add the parsnips and blanch for 10 minutes. They should be almost completely cooked, but not yet fork-tender. Drain and cut into chunks.

3. Melt the butter in a skillet. Add the parsnip chunks and cook over low heat, shaking from time to time until golden brown. They should end up tender but not mushy. Season with plenty of pepper and sprinkle with the parsley.

Serves 4

peas

S o you think you know what a pea is? A spherical green seed that grows in a group of other peas inside a pod. In order to get at the peas, you need to shell them, by splitting the pod into its two natural halves, which look like little sailboats. Indeed, in ancient Rome, they used the same word, *phasellus*, for a small sailboat or a kidney bean.* Ancient usage makes it clear that the word referred to the kidney bean and not the pea, which is *pisum* in Latin, whence the species name for the garden pea, *Pisum sativum*.

The word *phasellus* lives on in the species names of many other beans in the slightly altered form *Phaseolus*, as in *P. lunatus*, the lima bean.

Peas and beans both belong to the pea family, Leguminosae, because their seeds grow in pods (legumes)[†], and their roots form symbiotic clumps with bacteria that produce nitrogen.

Our vernacular terminology for the seeds of these very useful plants follows a logic of its own. There are, in normal parlance, three kinds of legume seeds: peas, beans, and lentils. Peas are spheres, lentils are small flat disks, but beans? It is not easy to define a bean. Yes, many of them are kidney-shaped but not all. Davidson essentially throws up his hands and defines beans as "any legume whose seeds or pods are eaten, and which is not classed separately as a pea or lentil." So if the legumes are not in the pea (*Pisum*) or lentil (*Lens*) genera, they are beans. All three groups of edible legumes can also be referred to collectively as pulses, the sturdy traditional English term (from Latin *puls*, a thick soup made from pulses, e.g., the mess of pottage for which Esau sold his birthright—conventionally said to be a lentil soup.)

All pulse seeds are dicotyledons. They develop from double seed leaves (cotyledons) into two halves that split apart easily when dried seeds are hulled. Split peas are the most familiar example of this. In India, dried pulses are called *gram* when they are whole and *dal* when they are split.

All that having been said, the only straightforward answer to the question "What is a pea?" is: A pea is a pea is a pea.

[*]The locus classicus for *phasellus* as boat is a poem by Catullus (Catullus 4).

[†]Latin *legumen* referred indiscriminately to pod and seed. In more precise botanic lingo, "legume" means the pod, or a plant with nitrogen-fixing root clumps whose fruit (the reproductive organ that holds the seeds) is a two-sided pod whose halves look like boats.

petits pois à la française
peas with lettuce and pearl onions

The lettuce protects the peas, keeping them moist and adding flavor.

4 pounds peas, unshelled

16 pearl onions, peeled

2 heads Boston lettuce, washed intact, then quartered and tied with string

10 tablespoons unsalted butter

2 tablespoons sugar

Salt and pepper

1 small bunch parsley, tied together or held by the original rubber band

1. Shell the peas and reserve in a bowl. Cut a shallow *X* in the root ends of the onions so that they will cook evenly. Cut the lettuces into quarters and then tie up each quarter with string.

2. Put 8 tablespoons of the butter with the sugar, ½ cup cold water, 1 teaspoon salt, and the pepper, produced by three or four turns of a mill, in a heavy enamel or stainless steel, 8-cup saucepan. Set it over medium heat and bring to a boil. Stir in the peas, then the parsley. Arrange the lettuce quarters and the onions over the peas.

3. Invert the pot lid or (to be like a French housewife of a long-forgotten era) take a soup plate that will cover the pot. Set either one on top of the pea pot and fill it with cold water. This will seal the pot and also cause the steam inside to condense back into the peas. Bring the liquid in the pot to a boil, then reduce the heat so that the liquid will barely boil when covered. Cook for 20 minutes, or until the peas are tender. During this process, replenish the lid water with fresh cold water.

4. Discard the parsley. Remove the lettuce leaves and the onions and set aside. Transfer the peas with a slotted spoon to a serving dish. If there is more than a quarter cup of water left in the pot, reduce it and then pour it on the peas. Scatter small pieces of the remaining 2 tablespoons butter over the peas. Correct the seasoning. Toss lightly.

5. Cut the strings of the lettuce and arrange the leaves around the edge of the dish. Put the onions inside this ring of lettuce. Serve immediately.

Serves 6

plantains

Plantains (*Musa* *paradisiaca*) are in the same highly ramified species as dessert bananas (*M. acuminata*). But plantains are starchier and need to be cooked, either when they are green outside and hard inside or when their skins have turned yellow and black, and their flesh is soft and sweetish. Their origin is Asian, but they came to the tropical New World via Africa, after half a millennium of naturalization there. Indo-Malaysian colonists brought them to Madagascar around 1000 and they spread westward.

In most of the Spanish-speaking New World, plantains are a basic feature of life, as purees or as chips. The chips go by a long list of names, depending on where you are: *tostones, platanitos, patacones*. The method is the same. Cut green plantains into angled slices. Fry until soft. Flatten them with a rolling pin or, better still, with a hinged wooden device purpose-built for the task, a *tostonero*.

Cultivated varieties of *Musa* are seedless and produce fruit without pollination, by parthenocarpy. The banana/plantain fruit is technically a berry (skin covering a soft inside). Another way of speaking about bananas is to call the individual fruits fingers, which grow in layers called hands or combs. There are 10 to 20 fingers in a hand and 6 to 15 hands on a stalk. The same plot of land that will produce 98 pounds of potatoes will grow 4,400 pounds of banana/plantains.

The leaves of *Musa* are very large and are used as wrappers for steamed foods in Mexico, Puerto Rico, and the Philippines.

*The genus *Musa* and its family Musaceae are often said to be named after Antonius Musa, physician to the first Roman emperor, Augustus. Musa, a Greek slave, was freed by Augustus, perhaps because Augustus did not die after Musa treated him with cold baths during a bout of typhoid fever. Why Linnaeus would have chosen to honor this savant by connecting him forever with an exotic fruit is hard to guess. No source I have found explains the anomaly. Doesn't it seem more probable that the Swedish father of binomial taxonomy, when faced with a fruit of the Orient, would have looked to an oriental source for the name he would bestow upon it? Indeed. And I would argue that that is almost certainly what he did.

Musa is a reasonable Latinization for the Arabic word for banana (*muz*). And the species name *paradisiaca* derives from the Islamic epithet for the plant, "tree of Paradise." In an Arabic myth possibly originating in India, the banana was said to be the forbidden fruit of Paradise. Sometimes it is called a fig, because of its large leaves, which, in the Asian/Arabic myth of Eden, amply covered the nudity of Adam and Eve.

migan de figues vertes
green plantain puree, french antilles

This is the spicy, hot staple of the French islands. It serves as an emblem of ethnic identity for the Guadeloupean woman protagonist in the novel *Un Plat de Porc aux Bananes Vertes* (1967) by André and Simone Schwarz-Bart. *Migan* is Guadeloupean patois for a puree. *Figues vertes*, green figs, mirror the Asian mythical identification of bananas and figs, perhaps because of East Asian laborers brought to the French islands.

4 green plantains

Salt

10 tablespoons peanut oil, approximately

1 bunch scallions, trimmed and chopped

1 tablespoon chopped chives

Black pepper

2 to 3 Scotch bonnet peppers, trimmed and seeded

1 medium onion, peeled and thinly sliced

2 tablespoons lard, pounded to a paste with 2 teaspoons annatto (achiote)

1. Peel and dice the plantains. Cover with lightly salted boiling water, lower the heat, and simmer until tender. Process with the steel blade until fairly smooth.

2. Heat ½ cup of the oil in a skillet. Add the scallions, chives, black pepper, 1 or 2 Scotch bonnet peppers, and salt. Sauté until the scallions just begin to brown. Then stir in the plantain puree. Add additional oil, if necessary, to produce a smooth texture, cover, and simmer over low heat for 5 minutes.

3. Meanwhile, heat 2 tablespoons of the oil in another skillet. Lower the heat, add the onion slices, and sauté until translucent. Then add 1 sliced Scotch bonnet pepper and the annatto-lard mixture. Stir until the mixture melts and combines with the other ingredients.

4. Mound the plantain puree on a serving platter. Pour the sauce from step 3 over it and serve hot.

Serves 8

Note: Scotch bonnet peppers, like all chiles, must be handled with care. Wash your hands thoroughly after touching them. Avoid rubbing your eyes or touching other sensitive places until you are sure you have removed all traces of the peppers.

mofongo

Afro-Caribbean food reaches its starchy apex with this spherical trademark dish. Mofongo is the Puerto Rican answer to Chinese pork buns. The soaking leaches out a naturally occurring bitter latex from the plantain pulp.

Lard

½ pound pork rind, cut into 2-inch squares and soaked in cold water for 2 hours

4 green plantains, peeled, cut on a bias in ½-inch slices, and soaked in cold water for 1 hour

Salt

1. Melt the lard in a heavy pot. Set the pork rind squares in the lard, fat side down. Cover and cook over low heat until tender, about 15 minutes. Remove the cover, raise the heat to medium, and fry another 15 minutes, or until crisp and brown. Drain off the excess fat. Sprinkle with salted water to make the cracklings (*chicharrones*) puff up.

2. While the chicharrones are crisping, drain the plantain slices and fry gently in lard until tender but not browned. Mash the plantain slices with a mortar and pestle. Add the chicharrones, salt to taste, and continue mashing so as to crush the chicharrones.

3. Form into balls about the size of tennis balls with your hands and serve while warm.

Serves 6 to 8

potatoes

The potato (*Solanum tuberosum*) is the most important vegetable in the world. Annual production hovers around 700 billion pounds. This is almost twice as much as the total for the number two vegetable, the cassava, and roughly triple production totals for the next three, which are, in descending order, the sweet potato, the tomato, and the watermelon. Four of these five are native American plants unknown in Europe, Asia, or Africa before 1492. The watermelon came to the Americas with the slave trade from Africa.

The next five are Old World crops (bananas, cabbages, grapes, oranges, apples), but the potato is king without rival. And given that it is familiar to every culture, there is not much point in my describing it to anyone likely to read this book. I do mean, however, to defend it against the inevitable snobbery that faces something cheap and universally available, even though it is very good to eat.

Just before the end of communism in Russia, I was in Moscow as a journalist and decided to cook dinner in the full-time correspondent's apartment with ingredients bought at an unofficial hard-currency market. I bought steak hacked from a quarter steer on a makeshift table. Then I looked for potatoes. The thugs who dealt in them were used to selling potatoes in 20-kilo sacks. I wanted six. Six potatoes. They laughed at me, handed them over, and refused to take money for such a paltry purchase.

So here, as a belated retort to those Circassian wiseguys, is the grandest and most splendid potato recipe thus far devised by human beings. Followed by two more down-to-earth but no less delicious potato classics.

croquettes de pommes
de terre dauphine
potato croquettes dauphine

These potato fritters are the high point of potato cookery, sitting atop a pyramid of advance preparation, none of it particularly complex except in overall conception. You start by making mashed potatoes, which you then beat together with egg yolk (and some white, too) to achieve *pommes duchesse*—Duchess potatoes, an appareil which, in the old cuisine, was piped through a pastry tube to form a scalloped circle around a roast or other platter-borne main course. Once you have pommes duchesse in hand, you tell your assistant to prepare a cream-puff dough (*pâte à choux*), essentially flour and whole eggs beaten together over low heat.

Finally (or almost finally), you beat together the Duchess potatoes and the cream-puff dough to make a *pommes dauphine* appareil. *Dauphine*, literally a female dolphin, was the French equivalent in royal rank of the Princess of Wales, wife of the heir apparent to the throne. The title comes from the Dauphiné, a region of eastern France whose main town is Grenoble. Although *dauphin* is the normal word for dolphin, the noble title has nothing directly to do with the aquatic mammal. The title originated as an emblem in the coat of arms of a local dauphinois nobleman. Its most famous bearer was the son of Louis XIV, Louis le Grand Dauphin, who died before his father.

Croquettes is now a naturalized English word. It comes from the French *croquer*, to crunch or make noise while chewing. So croquettes are little crunchy things.

2 pounds potatoes, peeled and quartered

Salt

11 tablespoons butter

White pepper

3 whole eggs

4 egg yolks, lightly beaten

10 tablespoons flour

1 cup dried bread crumbs, approximately

Oil for deep-frying

1. Preheat the oven to 400 degrees.
2. Plunge the potato quarters into lightly salted boiling water to cover and boil until tender but still firm, around 20 minutes.

3. Drain the potatoes. Set them on a baking sheet and dry them out in the oven for a few minutes. Hold the oven door ajar with a wooden spoon. Then put the potatoes through a potato ricer into a mixing bowl.

4. Beat 7 tablespoons of the butter into the potatoes. Season with salt and white pepper. Then beat in 1 whole egg and all the egg yolks. Set aside.

5. Prepare an unsweetened cream-puff dough (*pâte à choux*): Combine ½ cup water, 1 teaspoon salt, and the remaining 4 tablespoons butter in a saucepan and bring to a boil. Remove from the heat and add the flour all at once. Stir with a wooden spoon over medium heat until the dough dries out to the point where it no longer sticks to the spoon. It will also begin to leak butter. At this point, remove the dough from the heat. Stir in the remaining 2 whole eggs, one at a time, blending well.

6. Beat the cream-puff dough into the potato mixture. You now have an appareil Dauphine.

7. Using two metal soupspoons, divide the appareil Dauphine into lime-sized spheres or croquettes. While you do this, keep dipping the spoons in cold water to clean them. Collect the croquettes on a sheet of wax paper.

8. Dredge the croquettes in the bread crumbs and set them on a clean sheet of wax paper.

9. Heat the oil for deep-frying until it just begins to smoke. Lower the heat slightly and fry the croquettes, a few at a time, until they are golden brown. Drain in a bowl lined with paper toweling and keep them hot in a warm oven until you have finished frying all of them.

Serves 6

mashed potatoes

By a chain of circumstances too trivial to bother rehearsing now, I found myself in the dining room of the Auberge de l'Ill in Alsace with my two-year-old son Michael in the spring of 1967, on the very day that the restaurant received its third Michelin star. I hadn't intended to bring Michael along, but when Chef Haeberlin heard that he'd been left with his mother in the hotel, he insisted that I go get them.

But what did he intend to serve Michael? This was a place renowned for its *foie gras en brioche* and stag St. Hubert, not foods for a toddler. The chef, a parent himself, knew that well. First he sent out poached eggs, twin suns nestled in cumulus clouds. Michael looked at them with obvious delight and said: "Apricots."

It was an impressive observation, visually accurate and a sign of a large vocabulary in one so young. The next course taxed my own vocabulary. Haeberlin had announced he would make a *mousseline*. A muslin?

From a kitchen feverish with excitement over the sudden attention of the world came silken mashed potatoes worthy of their elegant French name, *pommes de terre mousseline*. I try to think of that moment whenever I hear adults clucking about their children's unadventuresome palates. A great chef knew that epicures are not born but bred, slowly.

On its native ground, high up in the Andes, the potato was not traditionally mashed. Descendants of the indigenous peoples of that hostile environment dehydrated their tubers in the mountain air; so they would keep forever and didn't weigh much. Rehydrated, *papas secas* go in soup or get chopped and fried. You do not find mashed potatoes in Cuzco next to your *cuy chactado*.*

But when the first round of globalization. d/b/a the Spanish Empire, brought potatoes to Europe, it didn't take long before cooks were boiling them until soft and then crushing them into a puree. The same civilization that had crushed a hemisphere took easily to turning hard tubers and other fleshy vegetables into malleable pastes smoothed out and improved in taste with fat.

You can tell that I am not one of those who admire lumpy mashed potatoes. I hold with Roy Finamore and Georges Blanc, godfathers of this recipe, in wanting to manipulate the potato so that it will remind us as little as possible of its solid, starchy, gluey nature. Cook over matter is my motto.

*Split grilled guinea pig, head still attached

2 pounds Yukon gold or russet potatoes, peeled and cut into quarters
   (or eighths if the potatoes are very large)
Salt
10 tablespoons butter, at room temperature
1 cup heavy cream, approximately
White pepper
Duck or goose fat (optional)

1. In a large, nonaluminum pot, cover the potatoes generously with cold water. Toss in as much salt as you can grab with the fingers of one hand. Bring to a boil and reduce the heat so as to produce a gentle bubbling.

2. When a fork slides easily into the largest potato chunk (start testing after 15 minutes of boiling), drain the potatoes in a colander and then return to the pot. Stir the potatoes over medium heat to steam out the excess moisture. The mashing comes later: You are interested here only in a relatively brief exposure to mild heat. Remove from the heat when you notice a thin layer of potatoes collecting on the bottom of the pan.

3. Dump the potatoes into a mixing bowl. Then put them through a ricer (hand mashers and food mills do not do the job as easily or as well; food processors tend to produce library paste) held over a clean saucepan.

4. Put the riced potatoes over low heat and beat in the butter, cut into small pieces, with a wooden spoon. When the butter has all melted and blended into the potato, start beating in the cream, a quarter cup or so at a time. Continue adding the cream until you have the consistency you want: More cream makes for silkier, lighter, looser, richer mashed potatoes.

5. You can stop here, after seasoning with salt and white pepper (black pepper will leave black specks in your pure white puree), and serve while still warm (this dish is not improved by holding, even in a double boiler, for long periods). But if you want to get the smoothest possible result, push the puree through a drum sieve (tamis) and, for an extra dollop of richness, melt in a couple of tablespoons or so of duck or goose fat.

Serves 6

pommes de terre anna
potato cake

This is best done in one of those round copper casseroles sold as pommes Anna pans. *Faute de mieux*, use a soufflé or charlotte mold with a 6-inch diameter. You end up with a potato cake formed with overlapping potato circles. If you were to intersperse the potato circles with black truffle circles you would be broke but happy with your *pommes de terre sarladaises*.

Who was the eponymous Anna? Pavlova? Karenina? I have no idea. But I've been to Sarlat, a picturesque old town in the Dordogne in southwest France where black truffles grow not on but under trees.

1½ pounds potatoes
12 ounces butter, clarified
Salt

1. Peel the potatoes and hold in cold water until you finish peeling them all. Then trim them into cylinders so that you can produce uniform slices.

2. Slice as thin as possible, preferably with a mandoline, or barring that, a thin sharp knife.

3. Generously butter the bottom and sides of the pan. Melt the rest of the butter.

4. Arrange the potato slices in an overlapping circle around the outer edge of the bottom of the pan. Then make a second overlapping circle inside the first. Continue until you have covered the bottom of the pan with concentric circles of overlapping potato slices. Sprinkle lightly with salt. Take a pastry brush and lightly coat the potato slices with butter.

5. Repeat this process, making several layers, but no more than six. Coat with a final layer of butter. Cover and bake in a 425-degree oven for about 30 minutes. The dish is done when a knife slips easily through the potatoes.

6. To serve, pour off all the butter you can (reserving it for future use). Either serve directly from a pommes Anna pan or unmold onto a serving plate: First, invert an ordinary plate over the pan or mold. Holding the mold with one hand and the plate with the other, flip them over so the potato cake ends up on the plate. Then slip the cake onto the serving platter.

Serves 4

rutabaga

t is a testimony to the power of our appetite for novelty that the lowly rutabaga (*Brassica napus*) has just now begun enjoying a moment in the glare of chic. In most of its lifespan, since it emerged spontaneously as a hybrid of two other Brassicas—turnips (*B. rapa* var. *rapa*, see page 234) and cabbage (*B. oleracea* var. *capitata*)—growing near each other in medieval European gardens, the rutabaga, aka yellow turnip aka swede aka rape, has occupied the unenviable position of humblest vegetable of them all.

We're concerned here with the unpopular, globular, galumphing, waxed root vegetable which, when peeled, cleavered into sections, and cooked in boiling water, will yield a perfectly agreeable yellow mash. Glamorous chefs are currently inventing clever new recipes for this maligned—and very cheap—vegetable. But the classic is the classic bashed neeps, a Scottish puree that has kept crofters north of the River Tweed warm against the winter chill. "Neeps" is their word for rutabaga (and white turnips), from the same root that gives turnips their second syllable: the Latin *napus*. As for "rutabaga," it's of Swedish origin, actually from the dialect of West Götland: *rotabagge*, or root bag. The rutabaga itself came to England from Sweden, which must be why they call them swedes over there (lowercase and lower class).

The same species is of ever greater economic and nutritional importance as the source of rapeseed oil, that politically correct, low-cholesterol cooking oil marketed for obvious reasons as canola oil. Rape is the Olde English name for *B. napus* var. *napus* or var. *oleifera*.

Rutabaga has a modest literary history. Ogden Nash once wrote*:

We gobbled like pigs
On rutabagas and salted figs.

Although Nash must have meant the combination to be a comical and unappealing pair, rutabagas and figs do have a fundamental connection as plants that are high in calcium and therefore recommended for those in danger of osteoporosis, but not for people prone to passing calcium-based kidney stones.

Former children of my generation with book-worshiping mothers may have been subjected to Carl Sandburg's *Rootabaga Stories* (1922), prairie fairy tales that are whimsical in intent, but leaden in effect.

---

*In *Family Reunion* (1950). Around this time, my wife's uncle Phil was Nash's tax accountant. Presumably he paid his bills by check, but he also bestowed autographed copies of his latest books on Uncle Phil, which contained little autograph poems appropriate for the occasion and their recipient. I am very fond of:

Philip Shan,
He knows where the money's gone.

bashed neeps
mashed rutabaga

1 pound rutabaga

4 tablespoons butter, approximately

½ teaspoon mace or nutmeg or allspice

1. Bring 6 quarts of water to a boil.

2. Meanwhile, quarter the rutabaga with a cleaver. Peel away the wax coating and the stem parts.

3. Add the rutabaga to the boiling water. When the water resumes boiling, lower the heat and simmer, uncovered, for 15 minutes, or until the rutabaga can be easily pierced with a fork. Drain and cool under running water.

4. Process, pulsing, with the butter and mace (or nutmeg or allspice) until smooth. Transfer to a saucepan, and heat over medium heat, stirring, to dry out the rutabaga a bit. When the puree begins to coat the pan, scrape it into a serving dish. Beat in more butter to smooth the puree further, if you like.

Serves 4

sorrel

John Evelyn, the great diarist and author of a treatise on salad (*Acetaria. A Discourse of Sallets* [1699]), wrote in 1720: "Sorrel sharpens the appetite, assuages heat, cools the liver and strengthens the heart; is an antiscorbutic, resisting putrefaction and in the making of sallets imparts a grateful quickness to the rest as supplying the want of oranges and lemons. Together with salt, it gives both the name and the relish to sallets from the sapidity, which renders not plants and herbs only, but men themselves pleasant and agreeable."

Sorrel is a weedy herb of the dock genus *Rumex*, which is also the classical Latin word for the plant. Virgil included it as "fecund sorrel" in the short list of salad greens and vegetables in his minor poem *Moretum.** He does not, however, mention its two main characteristics. It is overloaded with oxalic acid, a chemical that promotes gout and kidney stones. And this acid makes it very sour. Indeed, its name means sour, deriving from Old French *surelle.*[†] This is still a French slang name for sorrel. But the modern name, *oseille*, which is derived from surelle, has its own slang meaning, money, as in our "folding green stuff" or "cabbage."[‡] It is not to be confused with the Jamaican drink called sorrel, which is made from the red petals of the shrub *Hibiscus sabdariffa*, sold as *rosa de Jamaica* in Mexico.

Sorrel leaves should be blanched if they are old and sour. They can be treated like spinach or pureed into a green sauce. One version of this, in England, is simply greensauce.

[*]The list includes cabbage, beets, sorrel, mallow, elecampane (*Inula helenium*, a relative of the aster once cultivated for the medicinal properties of its root), chickpeas, leeks, lettuce, radish, and pumpkin.

[†]*Surelle* comes from *sur*, which survives as an adjective denoting sour. *Sur* comes from the German *sauer* (as, obviously, does "sour"), sour or acid (see sauerkraut, page 52). That sorrel was a popular food in rural England is reflected in the large number of vernacular or folk names for it: sour sabs, sour dabs, sour suds, cuckoo's meate (because it was thought to clear the bird's voice).

[‡]Other *argotique* terms for money: *fric, pognon, grisbi.*

schav
sour-grass soup

This Eastern European cold soup crossed the Atlantic with Yiddish-speaking Jews who had picked it up in Poland. Schav is the romanization of the Yiddish for the original Polish name for sorrel, *szczaw*. It is still sold in U.S. supermarkets with a Jewish clientele, next to the bottled borscht.

1 pound fresh sorrel
3 eggs plus 1 extra yolk
Lemon juice
Salt
Freshly ground black pepper
Sour cream

1. Carefully wash the sorrel leaves in several changes of cold water. Separate the leaves from the stems and hard ribs. Coarsely chop the trimmed leaves (you should have 6 to 7 cups). Tie the ribs and stems together securely in a bundle.

2. Put the sorrel leaves and the bundle of ribs and stems in a large nonreactive saucepan with 8 cups of water. Bring to a boil, lower the heat, and simmer for 20 to 30 minutes, until the leaves are soft and starting to disintegrate. Remove and discard the bundle of ribs and stems.

3. In a large bowl, beat the eggs and the extra yolk with a fork until the whites and yolks are just combined, Slowly beat in the hot soup. When 3 or 4 cups have been added, trickle the egg mixture back into the saucepan, beating constantly. Pour the soup back and forth between the pot and bowl to cool it more quickly. Let the soup cool and refrigerate until cold, Before serving, season the soup with lemon juice, salt, and pepper to taste. Serve with sour cream.

Serves 6

shad with sorrel

In foodie folklore, the reason for this classic combination of fish and herb is that the oxalic acid in sorrel will dissolve the tiny bones that make *Alosa sapidissima* a trial to eat. Not so. Tom Jaine, the British food historian, disproved this myth experimentally. He did not, however, go on to claim that the delicious recipe should be abandoned.*

2 pounds sorrel

1 tablespoon butter, approximately

2 teaspoons flour

1½ cups milk

Salt

1 pinch sugar

Pepper

¼ cup oil

Juice of ½ lemon

1½ pounds boned shad fillets

1 medium onion, peeled and thinly sliced

10 parsley sprigs

4 thyme sprigs

1 bay leaf, crumbled

1. Wash the sorrel in two changes of water. Drain in a colander.

2. Put a third of the sorrel in a heavy medium saucepan with ½ cup of water. Set over very low heat and let soften. Stir from time to time with a wooden spoon. When the sorrel has wilted and condensed, add half of the remaining raw sorrel and another cup of water. Proceed as before. Add the rest of the raw sorrel to the saucepan with a final cup of water. When all the sorrel has softened, cover the pan, bring to a boil, lower the heat, and simmer very slowly for 5 minutes.

3. Drain the sorrel on a tamis or other strainer for 20 minutes. Discard the water that drains out. Then push the sorrel through the strainer with a wooden spoon.

4. While the sorrel drains, make a blond roux with the butter and flour in a non-aluminum pan. Stir in the sorrel puree a little at a time. Cook slowly, over low heat, until the mixture thickens.

5. Meanwhile, sprinkle a shallow baking pan about as long as the shad fillets with salt, pepper, the oil, and the lemon juice. Whisk together and arrange the shad fillets in the marinade. Turn the fillets so as to make sure they are coated all over. Then arrange

the onion slices over them and sprinkle with the parsley, thyme, and bay leaf. Let stand for 20 minutes.

6. When the sorrel is finished, remove from the oven and keep warm in a double boiler or bain-marie. Preheat the grill.

7. Drain the fillets. Place in an oval gratin dish or other pan large enough to hold the fillets in a single layer. Set on the second highest level of the oven.

8. Grill for 5 minutes. Turn the fillets. Brush with oil and continue cooking for another 10 minutes at the next lowest level of the oven or until the flesh is just cooked through.

9. Spread the sorrel puree on a long serving platter. Then lay the fillets over the sorrel and serve.

Serves 4

---

*Shad are more famous for their abundant roe than for their flesh. H. L. Mencken once praised American women for being "fecund as the shad."

soybean

Soybeans can be eaten for themselves, as edamame, lightly boiled immature (green) beans, usually served in their inedible pod and then shelled at the table. Raw soybeans are, practically speaking, inedible. They contain lectins and protease inhibitors, which interfere with digestion. Boiling knocks these gastronomic thugs out of contention.

After heating, soybeans come into their own as food. They have the highest protein content of any vegetable (35 percent), and their amino acid balance is very close to that of meat, making them an extremely efficient and valuable nutritional source for vegetarians. Of Asian origin, soybeans are now the leading agricultural product of the U. S., where they are mainly exploited for their abundant oil and as animal feed.

Most of us higher mammals consume

ma po dou fu   203

soy as tofu or bean curd, a delicate solid that precipitates out of soy milk* in the presence of gypsum or magnesium chloride (sold in a seasoned form as *nigari* in Asian markets). I have done this at home, starting with water and beans. It is excessively simple, although something of a mess. My tofu was, I thought, brighter tasting than storebought tofu. But I am perfectly content to buy the equally protein-rich tofu omnipresent in markets and then to use it in one of the hundreds of recipes I like from China and Japan.[†]

*Produced by soaking raw beans in water, grinding them, and straining off the solid residue

[†]Deep-fried tofu is an elegant dish, in my view. My friend Madeline Lee thinks otherwise. She once called it "deep-fried nothing."

ma po dou fu

This is the signature dish of Sichuan cuisine. It is hot, simple, and rustic yet a showcase of sophisticated texture contrasts and forceful, hot, typical Sichuan spices. It is named after an apparently real restaurant cook in the Sichuan capital of Chengdu who invented it some time before the fall of the Qing dynasty in 1911. There are now many restaurants in Sichuan and elsewhere offering *ma po dou fu* in widely varying versions. This minimalist recipe is based closely on the one Fuchsia Dunlop learned during her studies at the Sichuan Institute of Higher Cuisine in Chengdu. If you recoil from fiery spicing, look elsewhere for dinner.

2 pounds bean curd, cut into 1-inch cubes

Salt

4 Chinese leeks (the long, thin variety called *suan miao*) or 6 scallions, trimmed

1 teaspoon Sichuan peppercorns

1 cup any flavorless cooking oil

¾ pound ground beef

5 tablespoons Sichuanese hot bean paste

2 tablespoons fermented black beans

1 tablespoon plus 1 teaspoon ground dried red chiles

2 cups chicken stock

2 teaspoons sugar

1 tablespoon plus 1 teaspoon soy sauce

½ cup cornstarch, dissolved in ¾ cup cold water, approximately

1. Bring 6 cups of lightly salted water to a boil. Add the tofu cubes and adjust the heat to maintain a slow simmer.

2. Cut the leeks at a sharp angle to produce 1½-inch slices or cut the scallions in 1½-inch segments.

3. Heat a dry wok and toss in the Sichuan peppercorns. Roast them over low heat for about 5 minutes, stirring to prevent burning. Their color will deepen a bit and they will give off a fine smoke. Dump into a spice grinder or mortar and grind to a fine powder. Sieve to remove any stems and set aside.

4. Put the wok over high heat. Add all the cooking oil and heat until it smokes. Slip the ground beef into the oil and stir-fry until it begins to brown. Reduce the heat to medium.

5. In quick succession, add the bean paste, stir-fry for a half minute, then the black beans and ground chiles, stir-frying for another half minute. Straightaway, pour in the

stock, mix well, and then add the bean curd cubes. Do not stir. To avoid breaking up the bean curd, fold it gently into the other ingredients or simply push it from the edge to the center of the wok. While you do this, work in the sugar and the soy sauce. Taste and add salt if necessary. Simmer for 5 minutes.

6. Add the leeks or scallions. When they have softened, gently work in the cornstarch slurry, a bit at a time, until the sauce has thickened to the point where it coats the bean curd. Stop adding cornstarch at this point.

7. Pour into a serving bowl, sprinkle with the ground Sichuan peppercorns, and serve.

Serves 8 to 10

spinach

Popeye had it wrong about spinach. *Spinacea oleracea* doesn't make you stronger. Instead of adding nutritional iron, it blocks the absorption of iron with oxalic acid, making you weaker. In some people, oxalic acid also promotes painful kidney stones. So popping cans of spinach down the hatch is not all it's cracked up to be in the comic strips. But what is?

In spinach's favor it can be said that this annual herb is so full of water that it may help in weight reduction. If you doubt this, consider that spinach can be steamed all by itself over low-medium heat in a covered pot. The heat releases water, and by the time the leaves have wilted, but before they lose their emerald green, they are sitting in a bath of their own water.

Continue the experiment further. Dump

the spinach into a colander. Let it drain. Then squeeze it. More water comes out. Then chop the spinach on a cutting board. More water comes out. In the recipe for the most famous of all spinach dishes below, the spinach is finally squeezed even drier by twisting it in a dishtowel.

Handled properly, in nonaluminum cookware, spinach retains its lovely green color. Its taste survives cooking. For a gratin with Mornay sauce, it is bulked up with cream and then covered with a white sauce (béchamel) enriched and thickened with grated cheese that melts under the broiler.

Philippe de Mornay (1549–1623) was brought up as a Protestant and became an adviser to Henri de Navarre, until Henri converted to Catholicism and became Henri IV. Philippe was influential in promulgating the Edict of Nantes, which gave important rights to Protestants (Huguenots). He survived the anti-Huguenot massacre of St. Bartholomew's Night on August 24, 1572. Dubious authorities claim he invented several major sauces,* including the one that bears his name.

Even the name itself is a matter of historical dispute. After he inherited the *seigneurie* of a small hamlet from an aunt, he began calling himself Seigneur du Plessis-Marly. and some say he changed it to Seigneur du Plessis-Mornay. The village seems to have disappeared over time. It does not figure in the roster of 200,000 place names maintained by the *Institut Géographique National*. In chefspeak, Florentine refers to dishes in which eggs or fish lie on a bed of steamed spinach and are napped with sauce Mornay.

*Béchamel, chasseur

épinards gratinés à la mornay
spinach gratin with mornay sauce

Salt

3¼ pounds spinach or five 9-ounce packages

4 ounces (8 tablespoons) butter

6 tablespoons flour

Pepper

Ground nutmeg

Sugar

¾ cup heavy cream

1 small onion and 1 small carrot, peeled and finely chopped

3 cups whole milk, scalded and simmering

½ cup freshly grated Parmesan cheese

½ cup Gruyère or Emmenthaler cheese, grated into narrow threads

2 tablespoons butter, melted

1. First, blanch the spinach. This will preserve the green color and wilt the leaves. Begin by bringing 4 quarts of lightly salted water to a full rolling boil. It is best to use an unlined copper saucepan of the type used for candymaking. The bare copper does an excellent job of keeping the spinach green. Enameled or stainless steel surfaces do well also.

2. While you wait for the water to boil, remove and discard the stems from each leaf and toss the leaves into cold water in a clean sink or large bowl. Spinach is often gritty EVEN WHEN IT LOOKS CLEAN. Rinse the leaves three times, shaking them in each change of water. Make sure no grit comes off them after the third rinse. If it does, rinse them again. Then drain them in a colander, shake them dry, and let them stand until the water boils.

3. Put the leaves in the boiling water. Keep the heat high so the boiling will resume as soon as possible. Do not cover the pot as this will promote discoloration. From the time the water comes to the boil, the blanching should take only 2 to 3 minutes. As soon as you think the leaves have softened to the point of fork tenderness, dump them into a colander and run cold water over them to stop the cooking. Stir to quicken the cooling. This impedes yellowing and keeps the spinach from taking on what Madame Saint-Ange calls a *mauvais goût*.

4. Handful by handful, squeeze out as much water from the spinach leaves as you can and set them on a cutting board. Chop them roughly and then put them on a clean

dishtowel. Squeeze out the rest of the water by twisting both ends of the towel. Proceed right away to preparing the finished dish. Waiting will not improve the spinach.

5. Melt 2 tablespoons of the butter in a medium saucepan over medium heat. When the foam subsides, add the spinach and stir for 5 minutes to dry it out some more. Remove from the heat. Toss in 2 tablespoons of the flour, and pinches of salt, pepper, nutmeg, and sugar. Return to the heat and stir for another 2 minutes. Remove from the heat and stir in the cream, gradually. Then set over low heat. Cover and let the spinach cook very slowly for 20 minutes. Do not boil. Remove from the heat and reserve in a bowl.

6. While the spinach goes through this final cooking stage, prepare the Mornay sauce. Melt 2 tablespoons butter in a 6-cup nonstick saucepan. Add the chopped onion and carrot, and sauté over low-medium heat for 10 minutes without browning. The result is a mirepoix, a classic appareil, or prepared instrument, used as an ingredient in many traditional recipes for adding flavor or texture that would otherwise have required an undesirable or impractical amount of cooking if the same ingredients had been added in to the main dish from the start.

7. Scrape the mirepoix onto a plate. Then, using the same saucepan, without washing it, melt 2 tablespoons butter over low-medium heat. When the foam subsides, whisk in the remaining 4 tablespoons flour. Continue whisking until the flour and butter have melded smoothly and the flour has cooked without browning, about 3 minutes. This is a white roux, another standard appareil.

8. Without waiting, pour the hot milk over the roux and whisk vigorously. Remove from the heat as soon as the liquid returns to the boil.

9. Stir in the mirepoix, then set the sauce over low heat at the edge of the burner so it cooks only in one spot. Cook for 30 minutes, scraping from time to time with a wooden spatula to make sure this thick sauce is not sticking.

10. Preheat the oven to 450 degrees.

11. Push the sauce gently through a chinois or other fine strainer into a 4-cup glass measuring cup. You should now have 1½ to 2 cups of sauce béchamel, the classic white sauce, which is the base or mother sauce (*sauce mère*) of a family of more complex sauces, among them Mornay.

12. Into the hot béchamel, stir ⅓ cup each of the cheeses until they melt. Finish with the remaining 2 tablespoons butter. Whisk the sauce until smooth.

13. Spread 4 tablespoons of the sauce over the bottom of an oval or round 6-cup ovenproof dish. Then add the spinach. Mound the top with a rubber spatula. Cover the spinach gradually with the rest of the sauce. Sprinkle with the remaining grated Parmesan and Gruyère. Then brush the melted butter on the cheese. Set in the oven for 5 minutes, or until the top melts. If it doesn't brown, run under the broiler as close as you can get it. Leave the oven door open so you can see what is happening.

Serves 6

squash

Cucurbita spp. includes a wide range of squashes, gourds, and pumpkins. They have been cultivated around the world from the dawn of recorded time and well before. Their genetic diversity is primordial and science has difficulty classifying them neatly. Roughly speaking, we can distinguish the pumpkins, round and often ridged, the long zucchini type, and the summer squashes, hard-shelled and often used as containers.

Nearly thirty years ago, my paternal grandfather coaxed the normally trailing vine of *Cucurbita pepo* to climb up a cherry tree and grow a pumpkin. It was not a very large or pretty fruit, but it was mentioned on the garden page of the *Detroit News*. Since then I have always thought I had inherited special insight into pumpkins. Lately, though, after looking into the subject more thoroughly (my research until this summer had consisted almost entirely of eating pumpkin pies and carving jack-o'-lanterns), I am not so sure. Perhaps more than any other edible plant, the common field pumpkin, which shines from every right-thinking American's living room window on Halloween, illustrates the clash between colloquial naming and official botanical nomenclature. And that is only the beginning of the pumpkin enigma. Although you may resist the vulgar error of thinking of pumpkins as vegetables, can you so easily adjust to the scientifically unassailable notion that these giant gourds are berries?

They are, formally, berries because they are fleshy simple fruits, formed from a single pistil of the flower. They have no stones or papery cores. Grapes, tomatoes, and blueberries are typical berries: They are fleshy throughout and their outer layer (exocarp) is a thin skin. The pumpkin, however, is not a typical berry because it has a hard rind. Along with its cousins, the squashes, and its second cousins, the melons and cucumbers, the pumpkin is a kind of berry known as a pepo (rhymes with cheapo).

Indeed, the pumpkin is the ideal type of pepo. You have noticed, of course, that pepo is its species name as well, but it is also the case that the vernacular name of the fruit, "pumpkin" itself, derives in a straight and provable line from the Greek word *pepōn* (πέπων). This hoary word has meant pumpkin or melon down through the centuries. It began, in Homeric times, with the basic sense of sun-ripened or soft, was extended to mean "soft" as a term of endearment,* but then settled down as the generic term for pumpkin.

But the pumpkin, you object, is not soft. It is not a summer squash picked before its rind hardens. No, it is a late-maturing, hard-edged squash. I pass over the pettifogging question of whether it is a squash or some separate category of

*Polyphemus addresses the ram to whose belly Odysseus clings as *krie pepon* (κριὲ πέπον) at *The Odyssey* 9.447.

cucurbit, since "squash" is an Algonquin term and, it seems to me, we only confuse the issue further when we try to define it too systematically. We ought also to avoid another nomenclatural puzzle: Is the pumpkin—our hard-skinned, orange field pumpkin—a winter squash? In horticultural practice it is treated like one, and it feels like one. But other varieties of the species *C. pepo* are summer squashes. And they grow in "bushes," not on vines. Without wishing to strike a chauvinistic note, I think it is fair to say that our gargantuan native American pumpkin does not seem to fit either the "soft, sun-ripened" pepo role or match its summery species-mates because it is a latecomer to a diverse and easily hybridizing European clan.

giraumonade
martinican pumpkin puree

Giraumon is the pumpkin of the West Indies, with orange flesh and a mottled green skin. The name is usually described as "Creole," an unhelpful sort of etymology that leaves open the possibility of either African or indigenous origin. Since the plant is itself indigenous, the likelihood is that its name is Carib or Arawak. The seasonings of what is otherwise a straightforward puree reveal the influence of France and the local larder (the chile).

2 tablespoons oil or lard

1 tablespoon chopped chives

1 garlic clove, peeled and chopped

2 parsley sprigs, chopped

1 pinch dried thyme

2 basil leaves, chopped

1 fresh chile pepper, chopped, or 1 dried chile, crumbled

1 pound pumpkin puree

1. Heat the oil or lard in a skillet. Add all the ingredients except the pumpkin. Sauté until browning begins.
2. Stir in the pumpkin. Mix well and serve as a side dish.

Serves 4 as a side dish

pumpkin pie

This is the canonical dessert at Thanksgiving dinners, even though pie baking would have been beyond the technical possibilities of the Pilgrims in their first harvest season. Really a custard pie, it has a dense, throaty gravity to it.

3 cups flour

½ teaspoon salt

1 cup (8 ounces) cold but not frozen lard, shortening, or butter, sliced into thin pats

3 teaspoons vinegar

6 tablespoons cold water

1 egg, for the crust

2 cups pumpkin puree*

½ cup heavy cream

3 eggs, lightly whisked

½ teaspoon allspice

½ teaspoon mace

½ teaspoon salt

½ cup dark brown sugar

1. Combine the flour, the salt, and the lard, shortening, or butter in a large bowl. Cut the fat into the flour with a pastry blender or two dinner forks. Keep blending until the dough is well blended but not perfectly blended. The ideal is often said to look like oatmeal, little flecks of flour-covered fat.

2. In another bowl, whisk together the vinegar, water, and egg. Blend this liquid into the dough a bit at a time until the dough gathers itself into a ball. Then divide the dough in thirds and put each third in a Ziploc bag. Squeeze out the air. Then, if you are going to make three pies that same day, refrigerate all three bags of dough. If you are saving one or both bags for a future day, freeze both. In other words, freeze for the future, refrigerate for today. Let frozen dough defrost in the refrigerator for several hours. Let well-chilled unfrozen dough adjust to room temperature for 10 minutes.

3. Roll out the dough to an 11-inch circle between two sheets of wax paper. Strip away the top sheet of paper. Then pick up the dough with the bottom sheet of paper. Flip it over onto a 9-inch pie pan. Press into the pie pan. Press the edge of the crust with the tines of a fork to make a pattern of parallel lines and to crimp the crust against the pan. Trim away the excess, cover with plastic wrap, and refrigerate.

4. Preheat the oven to 375 degrees.

5. Mix together the pumpkin puree and all the remaining ingredients to make the custard filling. Remove the crust from the refrigerator, unwrap, and fill.

6. Set in the oven on a baking sheet. Bake for 45 minutes, or until the crust has browned. The filling will seem set to the touch but it will not be completely done until it cools.

Serves 6 to 8

---

*Only people who wear Birkenstocks in the kitchen still make pumpkin puree from scratch. Even Martha Stewart recommends using canned, unflavored puree. But if you have a pumpkin to hand, you can bake it (after halving it, scraping out the seeds and the strings), cut side down, on a baking sheet, for 45 minutes, or until flaccid, at 350 degrees. Process the pulp and force it through a chinois. Taste it. If you like it better than canned pumpkin, you might even want to make some again one day.

soupe au potiron et poireaux
pumpkin and leek soup

Pumpkin soup is a classic home dish all over France. This soup is an obvious variation on potato-leek soup (see page 137), less dour, brighter, yet thicker.

3 cups well-washed, sliced leek (white and tender green parts)
1 pound pumpkin puree or 1 pound raw pumpkin chunks
Salt
Pepper
1 cup yogurt, sour cream, or heavy cream

1. Combine the leek and pumpkin with 1 quart of water in a large saucepan. Bring to a boil, reduce the heat, and simmer until the solid ingredients are very soft, about 20 minutes.
2. Puree in a food mill or processor.
3. Season to taste. Serve hot or chilled. You may stir in the yogurt, sour cream, or heavy cream before serving (at which point adjust the seasoning) or pass a bowl of it separately so that it can be dolloped on by individual guests at the table.

Serves 6

zucchini flower fritters

The height of summer in otherwise peaceful Maine towns is the only time when many residents lock their cars. This is to prevent well-meaning passersby from stowing surplus zucchini (also *C. pepo*) in their backseats. A far more refined thing to do if you are a zucchini gardener is to fry the yellow flowers in a light batter.

2 dozen zucchini blossoms, stems and pistils trimmed
5 tablespoons flour
3 cups milk, approximately
2 egg yolks, lightly beaten
Salt
Oil for frying

1.   Wash and gently dry the flowers if necessary.

2.   Whisk together the flour, milk, egg yolks, and salt to taste to make a batter. Add only enough milk to make a smooth, pourable batter the consistency of a pancake batter. Keep whisking until there are no more lumps.

3.   Dip the flowers one by one in the batter and let them stand for a half hour on wax paper. This lets the batter cling to the flowers so that most of it will adhere to them during frying.

4.   Heat the oil to a depth of 2 to 3 inches in a large skillet. Just as it begins to smoke, slip in a few flowers with a tongs. Too many at a time lowers the heat of the oil and keeps them from getting crisp. After a minute or so, lift a flower with the tongs to see if it has browned underneath. As soon as this happens, turn the flowers, count to 17, and remove them to a double layer of paper toweling to drain. Do not stack. When all the flowers have fried, dust them with salt and serve.

Serves 4

sweet potatoes

The sweet potato,

Ipomoea batatas, is in terms of worldwide distribution the most important of all tropical root crops. Indeed, it is the seventh largest of all food crops. Eighty percent of world production is in China.

I. batatas is indigenous to Andean South America. Evidence for it goes back to 8000 B.C. in a Peruvian cave. It spread across the Pacific to Polynesia before Columbus, perhaps on a raft of the sort Thor Heyerdahl built and successfully piloted on the same route in 1947. Linguistic evidence for this is just as persuasive. Davidson points to obvious similarities between the ancient Peruvian *kumar* and *kumala, gumala, umala,* words for sweet potato in various Oceanic tongues.

Spanish explorers, starting with Columbus, encountered the sweet potato in

candied sweet potatoes 219

the West Indies. They brought one of its Indian names, *batatas*, to Europe, where it was erroneously transfered to the visually similar potato, to which it is not related. In hispanophone America, it often goes by another indigenous name, *camote*. Hispanic consumers (and Africans) also eat a mealy variety now available in U.S. markets as *boniato*, which has white flesh and is not sweet. The soft, sweet variety with yellow flesh is the one commonly consumed in the U.S., where, to compound the confusion surrounding this plant, it is often marketed as the visually unsimilar yam, to which it is also not related (see yam, page 238).

Spaniards brought the sweet potato to the Philippines, and Chinese traders quickly brought it home to mainland Asia. Linguistic evidence cited by Davidson strongly suggests that it subsequently reached Japan by an island-hopping trajectory that began in Okinawa, where it is known as *karaimo*, Chinese potato. Okinawa is in the Ryukyu Islands. In the Satsuma peninsula of the Japanese island of Kyushu, *I. batatas* is called *ryukyu-imo* and, in the rest of Japan, *satasumaimo*.

In the U.S., the sweet potato reaches its culinary apogee on Thanksgiving. As "candied sweets" it is a canonical side dish in the canonical turkey-based menu. Some form of cranberry relish or jelly and pumpkin pie round out the meal, none of which was probably eaten by the Pilgrims at Plymouth at whatever first harvest feast they may have had. In this recipe, the sweetener is that fundamentally American corn molasses sold as Karo syrup. This product was created by the Corn Products Refining Company and issued to the public on May 13, 1902, in the light and dark varieties still sold today. Until then, housewives bought their corn syrup from grocers, who sold it to them from bulk containers. The origin of the name Karo is uncertain. It may either commemorate a food chemist's wife named Karoline or it could be a descendant of an earlier product called kairomel. Karo syrup is also a traditional ingredient in pecan pie.

candied sweet potatoes

8 sweet potatoes
Butter for greasing a 12-cup baking dish
⅓ to ½ cup light Karo syrup
3 tablespoons butter
8 marshmallows (optional)

1. Bring 4 quarts of water to a boil in a large pot. Put in the sweet potatoes and simmer until just soft enough so that a fork will penetrate them without serious effort. Drain, cool under running water, peel, and cut into ½-inch rounds. Preheat the oven to 375 degrees.

2. Grease the baking dish. Arrange the sweet potato rounds in overlapping rows. Pour the Karo syrup over them. Dot with the 3 tablespoons butter.

3. Bake for 10 minutes and then arrange the marshmallows on top, if you are using them. Bake another 10 minutes, or until the sweet potatoes have darkened and the marshmallows have collapsed and browned nicely.

Serves 8 to 10

taro

Taro, because it is the most widespread common name in English, is the shorthand I will use for all the edible members of the aroid family. The vernacular nomenclature for these tuberous plants that have spread throughout the tropics reflects the difficulty of distinguishing members of one taro species from another. Names vary from place to place, even though regular consumers do not confuse them in kitchen practice. All taros belong to the large family of the Araceae or Aroidae, which take their names from the arum lily of Europe. There are 110 genera and some 1,800 species. Edible aroids divide roughly into *Xanthosoma* spp. (tannia, tanniers, *yautía*, and *malanga*) and *Colocasia esculenta* (eddoes, dasheen, cocoyam, taro).

Dasheen seems to be a contraction of the French, *de la Chine*, from China. Taro is the name used in Hawaii for the tubers of *C. esculenta* varieties mashed into a mucous pulp for the indigenous national dish, poi.

All edible aroids must be cooked, so as to defang the acrid crystals of calcium oxalate present in all parts of these plants. Eaten raw, aroids cause pain in contact with the skin and can produce loss of voice. This is why the aroid *Dieffenbachia picta* is known as dumb cane. The crystals can even be lethal in young children.

alcapúrrias de jueyes
puerto rican crab fritters

The Caribbean, more than any other region of the Americas, shows the results of the world-changing Columbus landfall in its foodways. This makes sense, because the whole business started on the north coast of Hispaniola, now the Dominican Republic, where the first European settlement of any kind was established at Isabela by Columbus during his second voyage in 1493. Spanish settlement quickly spread to the other big islands, to Puerto Rico in 1508, Jamaica in 1509, and to Cuba in 1511. Transatlantic trade followed rapidly. After the conquest of Mexico (1519–1821), it was inevitable that transpacific commerce would begin. In 1565, the galleon *San Agustín* sailed from Manila to Acapulco. Its goods traveled overland to Veracruz and then sailed on other ships to Spain, after stopping in Caribbean ports.

This first global trade route famously brought gold and silver to the Iberian Peninsula and Europe, but more lastingly it cross-fertilized the agriculture of three continents. In most places, entrenched local foodways absorbed the new larder—Europe assimilated Andean potatoes, Mexico added pork and animal fat to its almost meatless Aztec diet—but the Caribbean islands, because their indigenous people perished almost entirely from European diseases and other disruptions to their culture, were a gastronomic tabula rasa. Into this vacuum, rushed the foods and food ideas of Europe, Africa, and Asia. Local foods remained as well. Perhaps no dish exemplifies this literal melting pot better than the *alcapúrria.*

I first encountered it on the beach at Isla Verde, east of San Juan and just to the west of the self-consciously post-African village of Loiza Aldea, on the north coast of Puerto Rico. These torpedo-shaped fritters, which resemble the carimañolas of Caribbean Colombia and Panama (see the recipe on page 65), are part of the large family of deep-fried oddments that evolved as adaptations of an African style of cooking to local possibilities. In the U.S. South, hush puppies substituted cornmeal for black-eyed pea flour. In Colombia, slaves made a dough of cassava. In Puerto Rico, cooks combined the native tuber with the plantain or cooking banana they knew from Africa (*Musa paradisiaca*)* or the indigenous cassava and filled it with the picked meat of crabs from the local mangrove swamps.

Other fillings are known, including chopped meat and chicken. But the crab filling is the one you encounter in stalls (*kioscos*) at Puerto Rican beaches. Even four hundred years after some clever African immigrant invented this dish, its improvisational quality remains clear. The starchy constituents of the globalized dough mixture still vary from kiosco to kiosco. In a study conducted for a master's degree in food science and technology at the Mayagüez campus of the University of Puerto Rico (thesis submitted 2005), Maridía Rosario Passapera, investigating bacterial contamination of alcapúrrias, collected samples at thirteen stalls and determined that seven contained mixtures of yautía and cassava (*yuca*), three were a mix of yautía and plantain, and one each contained only yautía or cassava. Although the yautía-cassava mixture would appear to be the standard variation, cookbooks invariably advise mixing yautía and plantain, which suggests that this is the "classic" version. The achiote-reddened lard is a substitute for the naturally reddish palm oil that would have been used in West Africa.

1½ pounds yautía or other taro, peeled
5 green plantains, peeled
Salt
⅓ cup lard
1 teaspoon achiote (annatto) seeds
2 tablespoons adobo con sazon[†]
3 tablespoons recaito[‡]
1 pound crabmeat
Pepper
Oil or lard for deep-frying

1. Soak the peeled yautía and plantains in lightly salted cold water for an hour.

2. Heat the lard in a small skillet and add the achiote seeds. Simmer briefly until the lard acquires a reddish tinge. Set aside to cool.

3. Put the yautía and the plantains through the fine grater of a processor or grate by hand.

4. Mix the grated yautía and plantains together in a bowl. Then pour the lard through a strainer into the bowl. Discard the annatto seeds. Mix 1 tablespoon of the strained lard thoroughly into the dough mixture along with salt to taste, 1 tablespoon of the adobo, and 1 tablespoon of the recaito. Cover and chill for 3 hours.

5. Heat the remaining lard in a medium skillet. Stir in the crabmeat and cook for 5 minutes over low heat. Season with the remaining recaito, salt, and pepper. Let cool to room temperature.

6. Assemble the alcapúrrias. Lightly oil a piece of wax paper approximately 10 by 12 inches. Take ¼ cup dough, place it on the paper, and pat it into a flat 5-inch disk. Smear a tablespoon of the crab filling over the center of the disk. Use the wax paper to roll up the dough around the filling. Wetting your hands, form the dough into a sealed tube. Set on a baking sheet covered with wax paper. Continue in this manner until all the ingredients are used up and put in the freezer for at least an hour.

7. Heat the oil for deep-frying until it just begins to smoke.

8. Carefully slide three of the alcapúrrias into the hot oil. Fry until golden brown on all sides. Drain. Fry the rest of the alcapúrrias. Serve as finger food.

Makes around 20 alcapúrrias

*M. paradisiaca originated in Asia and spread to Africa around the year 1000 with Indo-Malaysian colonists of Madagascar. In Puerto Rico, the post-African identity of plantains persists in their local name, *guineos*.

†A popular condiment sold in Hispanic markets catering to Puerto Ricans and Dominicans

‡Also available in Hispanic markets

calalu

Calalu is a West Indian soup made from the greens of *Colocasia esculenta* or *Xanthosoma* spp. (or even okra and amaranth leaves). Calalú is the Spanish form, Callaloo, the English spelling of a word perhaps borrowed by slaves from the indigenous Tupi word *caárurú*. Callaloo is also the title of a journal of African and African-American writing published by Johns Hopkins University Press.

2½ pounds taro leaves, blanched in lightly salted boiling water
   for 3 minutes, drained, and thoroughly rinsed
¼ cup palm oil or any other vegetable cooking oil except olive oil
3 pig's tails, cut into 1–inch rounds
2 pounds stewing meat, pork, or beef
4 scallions, white and green parts, trimmed and chopped
3 garlic cloves, peeled and finely chopped
8 okras, topped, tailed, and sliced in thin rounds
1 cup dried shrimp
1 to 4 dried red chiles, trimmed and seeded
1 tablespoon vinegar
Salt
Pepper

1. Put the blanched taro leaves in a Dutch oven.

2. Heat the oil in a heavy skillet and brown the meat in it, a few pieces at a time. Drain the browned meat and add it, batch by batch, to the greens.

3. Remove the skillet from the heat for a few minutes to cool the oil. Then return to the burner and sauté the chopped scallions and garlic until the onions are translucent. Scrape into the Dutch oven with the remaining oil.

4. Add the sliced okras, the dried shrimp, and the chiles. Then pour in enough water to barely cover the solid ingredients. Bring to a boil, reduce the heat, cover, and simmer over low heat for an hour, or until the meat is very tender. Top up the water level occasionally, if necessary, and stir the soup to prevent sticking.

5. Stir in the vinegar, correct the seasonings, and serve hot.

Serves 8

tomato

Lycopersicon esculentum is the poster child of the Columbian Exchange. Before Columbus, Europe had no tomatoes and therefore pizzas were all cheesy white. Pasta sauce as we know it was impossible. And on and on. Although the Andes most likely is the tomato's home ground, it came to Europe first from Mexico. The word "tomato" derives from Nahuatl.

For a while, in the modern history of the tomato in the West, taxonomy was destiny. As a member of the deadly nightshade family, the Solanaceae, tomatoes were shunned as poisonous. This prejudice persisted well into the nineteenth century and even later in some places, including the rural U.S.

More recently, now that the tomato is mass-produced in low-quality strains that resist damage during transit, it is possible to buy whole raw "fresh" tomatoes in any month. Although anyone who would purchase such an abomination should be an object of pity, no one forces anyone to buy "fresh" tomatoes out of season. During the season, the glut of wonderful local tomatoes should restore even the most ardent Slow Fooder's faith in the market.

gazpacho

The original gazpacho could not have been a tomato-based salad-soup. It looked, one supposes, like the white gazpacho with its grapes and garlic. The post-Columbian, tomato-based gazpacho still carries the mark of its old-fashioned ancestor, stale bread, as antique as the Roman legions who brought *ur*-panzanella with them to Spain and started gazpacho on its forward march to global fame and fusion.

½ pound stale bread, with crusts removed

2 pounds tomatoes, peeled and chopped

2 green bell peppers, seeds and white pith removed, chopped

2 garlic cloves, peeled

¼ cup white wine vinegar

⅔ cup olive oil

2 teaspoons salt

1 small onion, peeled and chopped

½ medium cucumber, peeled, seeded, and chopped, about ⅔ cup

1 hard-boiled egg, chopped

1. Soak half the bread in water, then squeeze gently to remove the excess liquid.
2. Process the bread, half the chopped tomatoes, half the chopped green peppers, the garlic, vinegar, oil, and salt until smooth. Chill.
3. Mix together the remaining ingredients and distribute them among serving bowls. Pour the chilled gazpacho over them. If the soup strikes you as too thick, dilute it a bit with cold water before you pour it into the bowls.

Serves 4 to 6

ketchup

When the Reagan administration announced it was going to classify ketchup as a vegetable so that it could inflate the nutritional totals for school lunches, a cry of outrage boomed through the land. Some wags pointed out that ketchup, or at least its major component, tomato, was a fruit. This was technically true, but in normal speech, a tomato *is* a vegetable. So why not count ketchup as a vegetable dish, just as we would count cauliflower puree as a vegetable dish?

Ketchup bashing goes back even further, to the Nixon administration. RMN ate cottage cheese with ketchup for lunch in the Oval Office. Nixon haters like me mocked him for it. When I discussed this with M.F.K. Fisher, she advised me to stop sneering at ketchup and cottage cheese. Instead, I ought to provide the president and the public with first-rate recipes for these potentially first-rate foods.

This superb ketchup recipe comes from the archives of the Home Restaurant in Greenwich Village. Home's proprietors, David Page and Barbara Shinn, are committed to traditional American food at its finest. They know that ketchup has a long international history, starting as a *sambal*, or condiment, in Malaya. And, with that in mind, they have created a ketchup that filters the flavors of southeast Asia through American farmhouse linsey-woolsey.

⅓ cup cumin seeds

⅓ cup coriander seeds

⅓ cup yellow mustard seeds

2 large onions, peeled and thickly sliced

2 tablespoons olive oil

1 cup red wine vinegar

⅓ cup plus 1 tablespoon (packed) dark brown sugar

10 garlic cloves, peeled

¼ cup capers, with their brine

¼ cup hot red pepper sauce

¾ teaspoon mild paprika

¾ teaspoon ground cinnamon

¾ teaspoon ground allspice

¾ teaspoon ground ginger

¾ teaspoon ground oregano

¾ teaspoon freshly ground black pepper

¾ teaspoon ground cardamom

Three 28-ounce cans whole tomatoes

Two 12-ounce cans tomato paste
Kosher salt and freshly ground black pepper

1. Preheat the broiler.

2. Dry-roast the cumin seeds in an ungreased skillet over high heat. Toss occasionally until lightly toasted, about 1 minute. Transfer to a plate to cool and repeat with the coriander seeds and then with the mustard seeds. Be careful that the spices don't burn. You'll know they're done when a toasty, nutty aroma rises out of the pan. Coarsely grind the seeds together in a spice grinder, or a mortar, or with a rolling pin on a cutting board. Reserve.

3. Toss the onion slices in the olive oil and broil them until charred, about 8 minutes on each side.

4. Transfer the onions to a Dutch oven or other large, heavy, nonreactive 16-cup pot. Add all the other ingredients. Simmer, uncovered, over low heat for 3 hours, stirring every 15 minutes to break up the tomatoes and to keep the ketchup from sticking to the bottom of the pot as the mixture thickens.

5. Let the ketchup cool at least to blood heat before pureeing, in batches, in a processor or blender. If the puree seems too thin, return it to the pot and simmer until it is as thick as you like it. This ketchup keeps well refrigerated for up to 4 weeks.

Makes 3 quarts

pa amb tomàquet
catalan bread with tomato

Outside the vast area of Spain where Catalan is the first language of most people (Catalonia, Valencia, and the Balearic Islands), Catalans get no respect. Compared to the Greek speakers they outnumber, Catalans might as well be Basques, as far as the benighted rest of the world is concerned. And yet they are a vibrant and influential people with an original cuisine that goes back to medieval times and before (as compared to the insular, backward-looking Greeks, whose cuisine is almost entirely a provincial version of the foods brought to Greece by their Ottoman rulers after the fall of Athens in 1456).

Pa amb tomàquet is a simple peasant dish that may well be the descendant of some pre-Columbian schmeer. But it has become an emblem of a civilization. In addition, it is one of the cleverest and tastiest of all simple concoctions. Scraping tomatoes across toast flavors the toast with a minimal expenditure of tomato. It colors the toast a rich red-pink, something like the color of romesco, the great Catalan sauce. Olive oil and salt complete this Mediterranean miracle in nothing flat.

6 slices crusty white bread, toasted

2 ripe tomatoes, halved

Olive oil

Salt

1. Rub the toasted slices of bread on one side with the tomato halves. You don't want to press too hard and juice the tomatoes. Soggy bread is not your goal, just bread nicely coated with tomato.

2. Eat the used tomato halves.

3. Drizzle olive oil over the tomatoed toast. This helps spread the tomato, tempers its acidity, and keeps the bread from turning mushy. So add the oil right after rubbing on the tomato. Then sprinkle on some salt.

Serves 1 to 6

sauce choron

Alexandre Etienne Choron (1772–1834), a French musicologist and pedagogue born at Caen, may not have anything to do with this tomato-tinged variation of béarnaise sauce. But if you have a better candidate for its eponym, I would like to hear about him (or her). Meanwhile, I prefer to imagine that Choron circulated in the gastronomically zesty Paris of his mature years, the heyday of Carême, the superchef; Talleyrand, host of hosts; and Brillat-Savarin, the philosopher of the table. Why shouldn't an eminent musical luminary have met these other proto-foodies, at the opera or in restaurants? And why shouldn't he have proposed it to some of his food cronies?

Béarnaise itself was a nineteenth-century sauce, first made at Saint-Germain-en-Laye outside Paris, in the kitchen of the Pavillon Henri IV, named after the greatest son of the Béarn country in the lower Pyrenees.

More recently, Paul Bocuse, standard-bearer for the nouvelle cuisine, served sauce Choron, traditionally an accompaniment for grilled meats, with his signature dish, a whole sea bass encased in puff pastry decorated to look like a fish.

4 teaspoons tomato sauce

4 teaspoons heavy cream

⅓ cup tarragon vinegar

½ cup dry white wine

2 tablespoons finely chopped shallots

2 tablespoons finely chopped fresh tarragon

4 teaspoons finely chopped fresh chervil

½ teaspoon crushed white peppercorns

3 egg yolks

½ pound unsalted butter, melted

Salt

Cayenne

1. Whisk the tomato paste into the heavy cream. Set aside.

2. In a heavy, nonaluminum skillet, stir together the vinegar, the white wine, the chopped shallots, the chopped tarragon, the chopped chervil, and the crushed white peppercorns. Bring to a boil and reduce by two-thirds, to a bit more than ¼ cup. Let cool.

3. Whisk the egg yolks into the cooled herb reduction and cook slowly over low heat, whisking constantly. When the mixture acquires a creamy consistency, because

the egg yolks have thickened, remove it from the heat and gradually whisk in the butter. Then whisk in the reserved tomato-cream mixture.

4. Strain through a chinois. Taste the sauce. Add salt if necessary and a small amount of cayenne. Serve while still warm.

Serves 6

turnips

White turnips (*Brassica rapa* var. *rapa*) with their purple-rose blush start out much prettier than they end up when peeled and cooked in stews or sautéed in butter. Raw, they also have a mustardy tang that gets lost after heating. This is not at all to disparage the ever-popular turnip, whose swollen taproot has been a standby of the world diet since antiquity. Because of its spiky taste and leafy greens, it was formerly confused with mustard. Indeed, the two plants have related names in Greek (*siNAPi* and *NAPu*) and Latin (*napus*), which are the ancestors of various words in Europe (French *navet*, Spanish *nabo*, Italian *navone*), and in Britain, where neep survives as the ordinary word for turNIP in Scottish and various other dialects. The same root (no pun intended) shows up in parsNIP and most likely in catNIP.

You will not go wrong by cutting raw turnip into very thin strips and adding them to coleslaw or serving them in a rémoulade sauce (see Céleri Rémoulade, page 75). The greens are a tangy alternative to all the other greens we wilt and serve. But it is the cooked turnip that has always taken center stage. Before the advent of the potato, it was the primary winter root vegetable in cold climates.

The glamorous treatment below shows the French temperament in fine form. The human hand "turns" (the technical term for this) the raw turnip into small "olives." This is not only decorative but shrewd and sly. Shrewd because it yields small and therefore quick-cooking nuggets of uniform size with consequently identical cooking times.* Sly because it may remind the sophisticated diner of that other duck classic, *canard aux olives*. But these are quite distinct dishes in the eating. Whereas olives, usually green and acid, clash fugally with the fatty richness of the duck, turnips in their blandness offer a more comforting, unassertive counterpoint.

Despite all these virtues, turnips have acquired a negative reputation, no doubt among those who had to eat them too often. In French theatrical slang, a failure, what we would call a turkey, is a turnip, a *navet*.

Anne Page, in a mixed metaphor in *The Merry Wives of Windsor* III. iv. 71–2, says she would rather be buried alive and pelted to death with turnips than marry Fenton: "Alas! I had rather be set quick i' the earth, And bowl'd to death with turnips."

Unmetaphorically, and cooked just to the point of easy penetration by fork, the turnip can be a treat.

*Some readers may recall a parallel scene in *Wuthering Heights*: "We entered together; Catherine was there, making herself useful in preparing some vegetables for the approaching meal; she looked more sulky and less spirited than when I had seen her first. She hardly raised her eyes to notice me, and continued her employment with the same disregard to common forms of politeness as before; never returning my bow and good-morning by the slightest acknowledgment.

'She does not seem so amiable,' I thought, 'as Mrs. Dean would persuade me to believe. She's a beauty, it is true; but not an angel.'

Earnshaw surlily bid her remove her things to the kitchen. 'Remove them yourself,' she said, pushing them from her as soon as she had done; and retiring to a stool by the window, where she began to carve figures of birds and beasts out of the turnip-parings in her lap."

canard aux navets
duck with turnips

One 4½-pound duck

1 pound white turnips, peeled and cut in the shape of olives

2 cups chicken stock

2 tablespoons salt pork, finely chopped, or lacking that, lard or butter

2 tablespoons flour

Pepper

A bouquet garni (1 bay leaf, 1 thyme sprig, and 1 celery sprig, tied together)

2 tablespoons butter

1. Take a high-sided pot just large enough to hold the duck, the turnips, and the stock so that the stock covers the turnips. Drain the duck and the turnips, and reserve the stock.

2. Melt the chopped salt pork (or lard or butter) in the pot. Add the duck and cook over low-medium heat for about 20 minutes, turning the duck from time to time, while it turns a rich golden brown, the color of a roast duck. Remove the duck to a plate.

3. Whisk the flour into the cooking fat from the duck. Lower the heat a bit and continue whisking until the flour turns a light brown. Then whisk in the stock. Season lightly with pepper. Bring to a boil, reduce the heat to a slow simmer, and cook for 12 minutes, skimming off the fat that rises. Strain the sauce through a chinois or other fine strainer to remove any burned solids.

4. Preheat the oven to 375 degrees.

5. Rinse out the cooking pot and pour in the strained liquid. Bring to a full boil and then, immediately afterward, place the duck carefully in the liquid, along with any juices that may have collected while it waited. Add the bouquet garni. Cover with a piece of buttered wax paper. Then cover with a lid and place in the oven.

6. Cook for 25 minutes. Check to make sure the liquid boils gently. Adjust the oven heat if necessary.

7. While the duck is in the oven, bring 3 quarts of lightly salted water to a full boil. Add the turnips and blanch for 10 minutes. Run under cold water, drain, and pat dry.

8. Melt the butter in a skillet and whisk briefly until melted. Add the turnips and sauté until they are nicely colored.

9. After the duck has cooked for 25 minutes in the oven, add the turnips to the pot. Cover again with the wax paper and the lid. Return to the oven and cook for another 35 minutes.

10. Remove the pot from the oven. Take out the duck, being careful to pour back any liquid from the cavity into the pot. Place the duck on a round, flat serving platter. Then remove the turnips from the pot with a slotted spoon and arrange them around the duck. Discard the bouquet garni. Keep this platter hot in a turned-off oven.

11. Degrease the cooking liquid as much as possible with a metal spoon. You should then have no more than 3 cups of sauce. If there is more, reduce at a full boil. Correct the seasoning and pour over the duck and the turnips. Serve straightaway.

Serves 4

yam

Whatever your supermarket may claim, the "yams" they have for sale are almost certainly not yams. The yam that am is an African tuber not at all related to the native American sweet potato, which is often marketed as a yam. The sweet potato (*Ipomoea batatas*, see page 217) is a small thing compared to a true yam, which has orange flesh and a fairly smooth, potatolike skin. *I. batatas* does have a white-fleshed variety, but it is sold as boniato and not yam. The true yam (*Dioscorea* spp.) is large, has white flesh (*D. rotundata*) or yellow flesh (*D. cayenensis*), and appears only in U.S. markets that offer the full range of tropical tubers. Even these Linnaean names incorporate the confusion that surrounds this extremely valuable plant. By one theory, the yellow and white yams are part of the

fufu 240

same "species complex," but, van Wyk points out, they do not have the same number of chromosomes.

As the species name implies, the yam owes its scientific name to the very influential medical botanist Pedanius Dioscorides, a first-century Greek born in Asia Minor who traveled as a doctor with the Roman legions in the time of Vespasian and published *De Materia Medica* in the 60s or 70s. When modern systematic botany honored Dioscorides by naming the yam genus after him, somebody blundered by adding the species name *cayenensis* to make up the binomial for the yellow yam. Cayenne, the source of the adjective, is and was the principal city of the Guianas. *Cayenensis* thus implies a South American origin for the plant, which started out in Africa and crossed the Atlantic with the slave trade.

This is a smallish blunder of no real harm to anyone, and less hilarious than the set of blunders that ignorant Europeans caused by mixing up Guiana and Guinea on the west coast of Africa, and then confusing both of them with India, compounding the original blunder that gave India's name to the Antilles. This is how the native South American rodent *Cavia porcellus* came to be called Guinea pig in English and *cochon d'Inde* in French.*

The word "yam" is also of West African origin from Fulani *nyami*, "to eat"; Twi *anyinam* "species of yam") or perhaps, originally, from yet another language of the region. French retained it as *igname* and Spanish as *ñame*.

Fufu, which appears in several West African languages (Ewe, Twi, Wolof), as well as in Afro-Cuban Spanish *fufú*, is the moral equivalent of mashed potatoes. This is not a glib comparison. As soon as African slaves encountered other starchy tubers in the Americas, aroids† (dasheen, eddoes) and cassava, they mashed them, too, formed the "dough" into balls, and called the result *fufú* (as they did and do in some places with the plantains they already knew from Africa).

*By a similar process, the large Mexican fowl *Meleagris gallopavo* came into English as turkey [fowl] and into French as *dinde*, a fowl from India, or *volaille d'Inde*.

†For a fuller discussion of these plants, see under taro.

fufu

2 pounds yams
Butter (optional)

1. Place enough water in a large pot to cover the yams amply. Bring the water to a boil. Put in the yams and simmer, uncovered, until the yams are soft, about a half hour.
2. Drain and cool under running water. Peel the yams and mash with a potato ricer. Beat in enough butter to make the fufu very smooth.
3. Form into fist-sized balls and serve.

Serves 4 to 6

select bibliography

Child, Julia et al. *Mastering the Art of French Cooking*. New York: Knopf, 1961.

Davidson, Alan. *The Oxford Companion to Food*. New York: Oxford, 1999.

Dunlop, Fuchsia. *Land of Plenty*. New York: Norton, 2001.

Everett, Thomas H. *The New York Botanic Garden Illustrated Encyclopedia of Horticulture*.
    New York: Garland, 1980.

Goldstein, Darra. *The Georgian Feast*. New York: HarperCollins, 1993.

Guérard, Michel. *La Cuisine Gourmande*. Paris: Laffont, 1978.

Helou, Anissa. *Lebanese Cookery*. New York: St. Martin's, 1998.

McGee, Harold. *On Food and Cooking*. New York: Scribner, revised edition, 2004.

Montagné, Prosper. *Larousse Gastronomique*. Paris: Larousse, 1938.

Saint-Ange, Camille Andrée Marie. *La Cuisine de Madame Saint-Ange*. Paris: Larousse, 1925.

Schneider, Elizabeth. *Vegetables from Amaranth to Zucchini*. New York: Morrow, 2001.

Schrecker, Ellen. *Mrs. Chiang's Szechwan Cookbook*. New York: Harper & Row, 1976.

Sokolov, Raymond. *The Saucier's Apprentice*. New York: Knopf, 1976.

———. *Fading Feast*. New York: Farrar Straus Giroux, 1981.

———. *Why We Eat What We Eat*. New York: Simon & Schuster, 1991.

———. *The Cook's Canon*. New York: HarperCollins, 2003.

———. *How to Cook*. New York: HarperCollins, 2004.

van Wyk, Ben-Erik. *Food Plants of the World*. Portland (Ore.): Timber Press, 2005.

index